Dear Heather,

D1456505

[signature]

Here's What People Are Saying About *Full Speed Ahead*

"A straightforward, engaging, and down-to-earth book for those desiring improvement in the quality and direction of their lives."

—Anthony Robbins
Author, *Awaken the Giant Within*
and *Unlimited Power*

"*Full Speed Ahead* is short, sweet, impacting and powerful. Joyce has written a practical and real-world book for just about anyone. If you're sick of being in neutral or just plugging away, you need to read *Full Speed Ahead*, with a pen in hand, and use this practical book as a real tool. You'll be impressed with Joyce's ability to make you feel 'Better than Terrific.'"

—Ray Pelletier
America's Business Attitude Coach

"It's like taking a Joyce Weiss workshop at your own speed after reading this book. Her ideas are fresh, uplifting, motivational, and action oriented. You will become driven by change to thrive in this outrageous world."

—Sue Shoemaker, Director Donor Services
American Red Cross, Great Lakes Region

"This book is for anyone looking for new approaches that impact your quality of life. Joyce Weiss can be your personal coach. Her workshops and book have strategies to help you transform your life permanently in this age of constant change."

—**Katherine Svedman**, Executive Director
American Society for Healthcare Environmental
Services of the American Hospital Association

FULL SPEED AHEAD

Become Driven by Change

To Achieve Your Personal and Professional Best

Joyce Weiss, M.A., CSP

FULL SPEED AHEAD

Become Driven by Change

To Achieve Your Personal and Professional Best

Joyce Weiss, M.A., CSP

Bloomfield Press
P.O. Box 250163
West Bloomfield, Michigan 48325-0163

First printing 1996

ISBN 0-9648560-6-9

LCCN 95-81460

Editing, design, typesetting, and printing services provided by About Books, Inc., 425 Cedar Street, Buena Vista, CO 81211, (800) 548-1876.

Dedication

To my parents, Sara and Joseph Morris, for encouraging me to march to a different drummer. Thanks for the trust and love you give to me, and the strength to help others find their own magic within themselves.

Acknowledgments

To my husband, Jerry, my dearest friend and business mentor who never holds me back as my multi-faceted career continues to grow.

To my children, Ron, Wendy, Jodi, and Brian, who give me the greatest stories to share with audiences. Your strength and internal drive make me proud!

To my sister and brother-in-law, Marcia and Irving Miller, for being my personal cheerleaders. Thanks for taking the continuous phone calls to help create the book's powerful and energetic title.

I love all of you very much and I hope I have made as much of an impact on you as you have made on me! Your support and energy are always a part of me.

To my marketing director, Rita Jones, whose dedication, work ethic, and warmth keep the business running smoothly. Thanks for challenging me daily and for telling me things I *need* to hear.

To my editors, Judith Share Saretsky and Greg Gersabeck, thanks for your talent and many hours of debate and dedication to this project.

Finally, to my audiences, clients, and loyal friends who kept asking me to write a book. There would be no book without your input and encouragement. Thank you for sharing your challenges and successes with me. You have made my career a total joy.

This book is for anyone who wants to do more than survive. *Full Speed Ahead* is for top performers who want to achieve their personal best. Enjoy!

Prologue

Too many people are content with merely surviving in this world. To find true happiness and success we need to do more than just survive in our professional and personal lives. We need to thrive. We must break through existing barriers and learn something new. We must embrace our freedom of expression and cherish our diversities. We need family environments that not only nurture our individual uniqueness and potential but promote that expression in the workplace and through all phases of our lives. We must become driven by change.

I believe life constantly provides occasion for growth and change fuels it! Failure and success are both powerful lessons. Life is truly a magical process of opportunities!

For this book I chose stories from workshop participants and my personal experiences that I felt illustrate how the human spirit can soar from challenge. I have included proven practical exercises that will help you recognize the tools you need and the skills you have to excel in this outrageous world. The world provides the challenges.

This book will make excelling easier by suggesting options to meet those challenges. Then you can proceed "full speed ahead" to achieve your personal best and soar above the rest. Top performers realize that the best can only get better and constant improvement is a habit for excellence, both at home and at work.

After reading this book please share it with a friend. Then write us with your own comments or stories. They may be included in a subsequent book. I hope this book helps you find more joy in your lives. Please think of me as your personal coach, encouraging you to get in the driver's seat and become driven by change to go full speed ahead.

Table of Contents

List of Work Sheets

Introduction

Have you ever made the following statements to yourself?

- I'm so stressed out that I don't know what to do anymore!

- If one more negative thing happens to me today, I'll scream!

- My boss doesn't understand my job. He/she keeps giving me more work. I'm only one person and I can't take it anymore!

- My family expects too much of me. I'm really feeling like a doormat!

- Work used to be fun. What happened to the joy I once felt?

- There's no time in my life for *me*. I'm on a treadmill and don't know how to get off.

It's no secret that our world is a pressure-cooker. To think about all the things that cause stress on this planet is mind-boggling. So what is a person to do? Not think about it? To shy away from one's rightful share of success and happiness in this world is to merely survive.

The aim of this book is to help you gain the control you need to excel in all areas of your life. Completing the accompanying exercises at each chapter's end will help you to put more joy, fun, and creativity into your life. You will learn techniques to help you tap into your potential to create the kind of life you want. That life lies within you—maybe deep within you—but it *is* there.

All the great men and women of our times have been no different from you and me. They have found a way to reach deep within themselves and generate the courage, wisdom, and strength to create their place in history.

As a professional speaker, I have the opportunity to interview hundreds of people at my workshops. They have shared different insights as they deal with specific challenges they face, and how they resolve them. These people come from all walks of life. Some work for the government, some as educators, in management, and on the front line, some in corporate settings, others at home. I interviewed anyone who was willing. I considered each question I asked and will share the fantastic ideas I found along the way.

When I get a chance to walk on the beautiful beaches of the world, I look at the powerful waves and compare them to us. Like the mighty ocean, we *all* have magnificent potential within. The same types of treasures and mysteries within *its* depths are within *our* depths. Life's answers lie inside each of us. Everything we need we have! This book will help you explore your potential. You do have control; you do have choices.

In my workshops I love to use this catchy phrase: *The magic inside you is no hocus pocus. Set your goals and you create the focus.* Magic has been defined as a process to unveil the potential that resides and operates within each of us. American writer Ralph Waldo Emerson said, "What lies behind us and what lies before us are tiny matters compared to what lies within us."

You may be saying to yourself, "Yeah, yeah, this sounds good, but how can I make it work for me? How can I overcome my daily challenges and add joy and creativity to my life? How can I break free from daily routines and self limiting boundaries? How can I achieve my personal best?" This book explores the answers to those questions.

Chapters 1 and 2 address how to gain control while living a stressful life full of daily demands—how to balance those challenges and deal with the resulting worry, failure, burnout, and adversity.

Chapters 3 and 4 will show you how to have more fun at work and at home. The strategies will be apparent; you can put these ideas to work immediately!

In Chapter 5 we discuss how to communicate your ideas. It covers active listening and networking to help you meet new people who will enhance your spirit.

Chapter 6 deals with how to appreciate others' uniqueness and differences. Cultural diversity is a hot topic today. *Managing The Diverse Workplace* is the title of a workshop I've been presenting for several years. The horror stories I hear from people who experience prejudice and discrimination on the job are mind-boggling. We will cover the importance of appreciating the differences in others—differences in age, gender, sexual preference, physical and mental abilities, cultural backgrounds, educational levels, communication styles, and so on. You will expand your understanding of how your personal creativity can grow when surrounded by people with backgrounds unlike your own.

Chapter 7 deals with mental blocks that stop our creativity. You will learn to use your imagination and originality to celebrate the magic within.

Chapter 8 discusses risk-taking and realizing goals. We will tie these ideas together and help you integrate this information into your day-to-day lives.

I encourage you to start a notebook of "keeper ideas" that hit home. Personalize them to fit your needs (personal names, places, etc.). Keep this notebook with you and refer to it throughout the day as you develop strategies to help you go "full speed ahead." (We have included an Action Plan after each chapter to help you get started.) In today's world, we are bombarded by a staggering amount of information via television, radio, books, audio and video cassettes, and on-line computer programs. We often experience information overload. Fifty years ago novelist Gertrude Stein wrote, "Everyone gets so much information all day long that they lose their common sense." What would she think today?

Your personal action plan will use immediate "keeper ideas," help you focus on your goals, and allow you to gain more control over your life. You will be able to more clearly see all of the many choices which are available to you.

I will share with you ideas I have learned from my resources and life experiences, and, most importantly, from the many wonderful people I have met.

You may already use some of these ideas. Some concepts may not work for you, others will. Select the ones that speak to you. The main point is to help you gain awareness that your life *can* be better. The choices we make every day determine what kind of life we live. We already have many answers. Use this book as a catalyst to help you discover solutions that are right for you. Then you can put more joy and creativity into your life and find the happiness and satisfaction you deserve.

American inventor Charles Kettering wrote, "You will never stub your toe standing still. The faster you go, the more chance there is of stubbing your toe, but the more chance you have of getting somewhere." Let's get moving toward the kind of life you want.

# Chapter 1

Gaining Control:
Put Yourself in the Driver's Seat

Let us begin by discussing some challenges others have shared with me. A good warm-up question I ask at the beginning of my workshops is, "How can you guarantee you *won't* have any joy or creativity in your life?" Think about how you would answer this question. Here are a few typical responses

- "Kill every idea."
- "Only listen to negative news."
- "Never read the comic strips."
- "Hang out with people who complain all the time."
- "Never meet anyone new."
- "Do your daily work and chores and never take time for yourself."
- "Stay with a job that gives you ulcers and headaches."

- "Don't pursue hobbies."
- "Only see the negative side of family and friends."
- "Look at the devastation and despair in this world, and ignore the beauty and wonder."
- "Don't see the curiosity in children or the wisdom of senior citizens."
- "Only discuss sickness and problems."

Had enough? Take a deep breath, then exhale—forcing all those negative statements out of your body. Now inhale deeply, filling your lungs with oxygen and the fresh air of positive energy. It is vitally important to keep negativity to a minimum. Countless people have wasted their lives complaining about the dilemmas we all experience; they've done nothing to change their negative energy and behavior into personal positive experiences.

Our challenge is to look for the positive, to find opportunity in adversity. Many of you may already be doing this; my hat goes off to you, and to any eternal optimists who are reading this book. The fact is that some people have a difficult time adopting a positive attitude. You may be asking yourself, "How can I thrive and keep my optimism in such a negative world or workplace?" In this chapter, we will discuss five strategies which can help you deal with the daily challenges of life:

1. Put thoughts into action—take appropriate steps to reach your goals.

2. Be accountable versus blaming others—accept responsibility for your decisions.

3. Accept differences in others instead of judging them.

4. Welcome the challenge of change—prepare for fluctuation and reorganization.

5. Project a positive outlook because attitudes are contagious.

Strategy 1: Put Thoughts into Action

We all face challenges in life. Sometimes these challenges keep us stuck in unhappy situations. These predicaments can include burnout, corporate down-sizing, illness, boredom, divorce, competition, and financial changes, just to name a few. Remember, we choose how we cope with challenges. Different people react differently to similar situations, some better than others.

17th century French philosopher and writer Voltaire compared life to a game in which each player must accept the cards dealt. Once in hand, he or she alone can decide how to play those cards to win the game. Shakespeare said, "Life breaks all of us. Some of us get stronger at the breaks."

We can choose to dwell on our problems or go on with life. Take time to mourn a loss: a loved one who has died, a job lost to down-sizing, a marriage torn apart, or any other significant change in your life. We need a certain amount of time to heal. It is important to deal with the stages of loss and then move on.

Strategy 2: Accept Responsibility

We have the ability to choose our responses to difficult situations. It is our choice whether we live a boring, unfulfilled, miserable life or a life full of joy, contentment, and growth.

Some people blame their parents, boss, mate, etc. They don't accept responsibility for their own lives. A familiar meditation from a 16th century monk states, "Grant me the serenity to accept the things I cannot change, the courage to change the things I can, and the wisdom to know the difference." Some individuals find it easy to complain and blame. Here is a simple, effective question to pose to those who dwell on negative situations and don't accept responsibility. Ask them, "Now that you recognize the problem, what are you going to do about it?"

After I earned my Masters Degree in Guidance and Counseling, many people called me to complain about their partner or job. I listened and empathized, until I realized that many were bright, loving people who complained for years but never made any changes. I began to respond with, "I've listened and you have a legitimate complaint. Now my question to you is, 'What are you going to do about it?'" A lot of phone calls ceased. It was no longer fun for the complainers to look to themselves for solutions. It is vitally important as spouses, friends, bosses and parents to tell the important people in our lives what they *need* to hear, not what they *want* to hear.

While presenting a workshop to a Fortune 500 company, management told me what they tell all new employees. They suggest that new staffers look at constructive feedback as a gift, and not become defensive or insecure about it. What an incredible message! Accepting responsibility for your actions, and moving on when you feel stuck are two important lessons to learn when dealing with challenge.

Strategy 3: Accept Differences in Others

Learning to accept differences in others without judging them is another vital lesson. You might be thinking, "I'm a fair person, I don't judge people." But have you ever caught yourself saying:

- "You should have known better!"
- "I can't believe you did that!"
- "Why did you quit your job when you had all those benefits?"
- "How could you possibly date that person?"
- "What do you mean you don't drink!"

- "Chill out and join the party!"
- "Tofu? How disgusting!"

These are examples of subtle and not so subtle ways of judging others. The minute words like "should," "could," or "why" creep into the conversation, look out! These words shout: "Be like me, because different from me is wrong!" Pay close attention to your words . . . work to become nonjudgmental. We are beginning to learn the importance of taking action, accepting responsibility, and accepting differences.

Strategy 4: Welcome the Challenge of Change

Change is inevitable in this fast-paced world. Some major changes in our lives relate to health, jobs, relocation, a new boss or coworker, death of a loved one, or divorce. Minor changes could be the weather, your hair style, new eyeglasses or contacts. These minor changes may seem insignificant, but they affect us every day.

British musician and composer John Lennon said, "Life is what happens to you while you're busy making other plans." French novelist Victor Hugo wrote, "The future has several names. For the weak, it is impossible. For the faint-hearted, it is the unknown. For the thoughtful and valiant, it is ideal." And Will Rogers, noted American author, actor, and down-home philosopher, said, "Those were great old days! But darn it, any old days are great old days, even the tough ones. After they are over you can look back with great memories." So much change has occurred in such a relatively short time! When you think about it, the only person who really likes change is a baby with a wet diaper.

Participants in my workshops sometimes complain when I ask them to change seats and find new partners for an exercise. They groan, "Do we have to?" or

"I like my space!" These activities challenge their comfort zones. Yet others thrive on change and love to be paired with new people. Courageous people face the fear of change.

Be prepared for change. Flexible people will succeed better. A classic example of flexibility is in the popular Aesop fable, *The Oak And The Reed*. A proud oak tree grew on the banks of a stream. For a hundred years it withstood the buffeting of the winds. Then one day a violent storm felled the great oak with a mighty crash into the swollen river and carried it toward the sea. The oak tree came to rest on the shore where some reeds were growing. The tree was amazed to see the reeds standing upright. "How did you manage to weather that terrible storm?" the Tree asked. "I have stood up against many a storm, but this one was too strong for me." "That's just it," replied the Reed. "All these years you have stubbornly pitted your great strength against the wind. You were too proud to yield a little. I, on the other hand, knowing my weakness, didn't resist. The harder the wind blew, the more I humbled myself, so here I am!"

Start with a little change at a time. Alter just a few small habits daily. For example, listen to a new radio station, watch a new TV program, or read a different newspaper. Go out to lunch with a new friend or different coworker. Raise your standards when you want to change. It's time to modify the limited belief that you've always done it a certain way before, and therefore you can't change.

We cannot change a habit by simply talking. We must take action. If you want your life to improve, you must adjust your daily routines.

Each time I want to make a change in an aspect of my behavior, I do the following exercise. I put 10 pennies in my right pocket in the morning. Each time I notice I am using a new skill or breaking an old habit, I move a penny to my left pocket. At the end of the day I count the pennies in each pocket and review the actions I took to change my habit. This is an easy exercise. The results are obvious, the rewards uplifting. I stopped using the expression "you know" by doing this. It works!

The best advice we can give future generations, our children or coworkers, is to constantly upgrade our skills. Keep your resume updated and be flexible. When my children were young, I met a little girl named Susie who was afraid of bearded men. Since she was starting nursery school her mom took her to meet the mothers and children in the car pool, to prepare her so she wouldn't be afraid. Wouldn't you know it, on day one, one mother became ill and sent her husband to pick up the children. He had a full-grown beard. Even though Susie's mom tried to prepare her, change is constant and inevitable, and Susie had to confront her fear. We must all learn to adapt to change. Susie surely did. She grew up and married a man with a full beard.

When you find yourself doing well and are satisfied in a personal or business-related situation, challenge yourself and ask how you can do better. People lose out when they think they have achieved their goals and don't need to improve or prepare. We will cover this more in chapter 8.

Strategy 5: Attitudes Are Contagious— Is Yours Worth Catching?

If you add up all the challenges we experience in life you can boil them down to one word, the "a" word—attitude. A good, positive attitude goes a long way toward a happy, fulfilled life.

One of my favorite movies is *Forrest Gump*. The story covers the life of a 30-year-old man with an IQ of 75. His mother told him, "You can be anything you want to be." When Forest Gump's girl friend asked, "What are you going to be?," Forest replied, "Aren't I going to be me?"

Poet Douglas Malloch wrote in his poem *Be The Best Of Whatever You Are:* "If you can't be a highway, then be a trail. If you can't be the sun, be a star. It isn't by size that you win or you fail. Be the best of whatever you are!"

Rudy Ruettiger comes to mind when I think of individuals who achieve their personal best and never give up on their dreams. Rudy graduated from the University of Notre Dame in 1976. Why is he so special? As a kid he had a dream—a dream of playing football for this prestigious school. Rudy graduated from high school with terrible grades and very little athletic ability. Family and friends laughed at him for stubbornly holding on to his dream. Yet Rudy had a vision and decided to fight for the right to play for Notre Dame.

Rudy's next few years consisted of working with his father and brother in the steel mills because "the Ruettigers don't go to college." Then Rudy decided to attend a junior college, where he met a priest, who promised Rudy he would pay his tuition if he strived hard and received excellent grades. After much work Rudy was finally accepted to Notre Dame. He tried out for the football team and was repeatedly rejected. The coach thought Rudy was too short and lacked the necessary skills. But this did not dampen Rudy's enthusiasm, he wanted to play football! So Rudy showed up for every tryout session. Finally the coach relented and let him join the team. The coach had never met a player who wanted something as badly as Rudy did.

During the football season, the coach never allowed Rudy to play in a regular game, only during practice sessions. In the last game of the season the players pressured the coach to put Rudy in. He made a tremendous play that actually won the game, the only game that Rudy was ever allowed to play. Rudy's teammates respected his perseverance, tenacity and his work ethic. At the end of the game they carried Rudy, their hero, off the field on their shoulders. This happened in 1976, and since then, no other player has been carried off the field in such a manner. What a story of a young man who stood tall against the odds and wouldn't take *no* for an answer. My daughter, Wendy, introduced me to this inspirational movie, and to the novel, written by James Ellison. I recommend it highly when your morale and motivation need a boost to go full speed ahead.

Greek philosopher Aristotle wrote, "We are what we repeatedly do. Excellence then is not an act, but a habit." British writer Somerset Maugham penned, "If you refuse to accept anything but the best, you often get it."

Find your special uniqueness. Stay away from people who put you down and try to stop you from reaching your dreams and fulfilling your potential.

We need to stop saying "I can't" and "it's impossible"—words which limit us and stop us from being creative. These words promote failure. Pogo, the cartoon character, may be right when he says, "I have found the worst enemy and it is me." French emperor and military strategist Napoleon said, "Impossible is a word to be found only in the dictionary of fools."

Playwright Neil Simon said, "Don't listen to those who say it's not done that way. Maybe it's not, but maybe you'll do it anyway. Don't listen to those who say you're taking too big a chance. Michelangelo would have painted the floor of the Sistine Chapel, and it would surely be rubbed out today."

We have many choices on how to live our lives. Some choose to live negative lives, while others choose to change and improve. Some create their future and others wait endlessly. People who invest time in reading about personal growth create their futures! Optimists realize they have options to help find solutions. Optimists see the opportunities that life provides. They know they need to change constantly and improve to go full speed ahead!

When you meet your next challenge, think about your greatest obstacle or handicap. Could it be fear? What is your greatest mistake? Is it to give up? What is your greatest insult? Is it finding fault with others? What is your greatest gift? Is it forgiveness? And what is your greatest day? It is today!

Work Sheet
Chapter 1

Gaining Control:

1. What situations are most stressful at work or at home? _____
   _____
   _____
   _____

2. When I feel upset how do I typically react?
   _____
   _____
   _____
   _____

3. What upcoming situations do I feel may be stressful?
   _____
   _____
   _____
   _____

4. Which people cause me to experience stressful feelings?
   At work: _____
   _____
   Outside work: _____
   _____

5. What things do these people do that I find most unpleasant? _____
   _____
   _____
   _____

6. What can I do to prepare myself for these stressful situations (avoid, alter, or accept)?

_____

_____

_____

_____

Action Plan
Chapter 1

Gaining Control:
Put Yourself in the Driver's Seat

When you discover new ideas, or ways of performing a task better, write them down. It has been found that if new ideas aren't used within 24 hours, they are generally forgotten. Make a copy of this plan and place it in a prominent location in your home or office. Make sure you try all of the things you have made note of.

1._____
2._____
3._____
4._____
5._____

Top performers are people who never run out of options. They look at challenges by searching for another solution. Top performers use problem-solving tools to help generate ideas. They do not complain or blame others. What solutions have you shared with your family or company?

_____
_____
_____
_____
_____
_____
_____

Chapter 2

Stress: Re-charge Your Battery by Channeling Stress into Positive Energy

Do you ever wonder how you made it through the day? People have their own daily set of challenges and situations that evoke stress. You cannot avoid stress. It's a tangible energy that resides in the mind and body of all human beings, even babies. Have you ever heard infants cry for milk when they are hungry? Tell me that is not stress.

Would you like to feel more energized and gain more control over your busy life? If so, read on.

In ancient times, the wind meant great trouble for human beings. It constantly blew down their structures, put out their fires, and generally, was a pain in the neck. People realized that the mighty winds were inevitable—a force of nature that could not be stopped—so they began to deal with it. As they learned more about it, they discovered they could use the power of the wind for windmills and sailing boats. Today, we are finding new ways to channel the wind into a force of positive change for this planet. Think of the stress in your life as the wind. In this chapter you will learn how to channel that stress into positive energy.

People today are constantly striving to achieve more balance in their lives. Participants in my stress management workshops often vent their frustrations about not enjoying their work and not having enough time for their families or themselves. Sometimes we are so busy making a living that we forget how to live!

Author Natasha Josefowitz wrote the following in her book *Is This Where I Was Going?*:

> I have not seen the plays in town
> only the computer printouts
>
> I have not read the latest books
> only *The Wall Street Journal*
>
> I have not heard birds sing this year
> only the ringing of phones
>
> I have not taken a walk anywhere
> but from the parking lot to my office
>
> I have arrived
> Is *this* where I was going?[1]

Think of this scenario for your own life. If your bank credited your account each morning with $86,400, carried no balance from the previous day, allowed you to keep no cash in your account, and each day canceled the amount you failed to use during that day, what would you do? You would probably draw out every cent each day. You have such a bank and its name is *time*. Every morning it credits you with 86,400 seconds. It carries over no balances. It allows no overdrafts. Each day it opens a new account for you. Each night it burns the records of that day. If you fail to use each day's deposit, the loss is yours. There is no going back. There

---

[1]Reprinted by permission of Warner Books/New York from *IS THIS WHERE I WAS GOING?* copyright © 1983 by Natasha Josefowitz.

is no borrowing against tomorrow. You live in the present on today's deposit. Invest so as to get the utmost in health, happiness, and success. Remember our earlier statement. Many people are so busy making a living they don't know how to make a life.

My favorite definition of stress is: a state of emotion or time when you don't take care of your own needs. It doesn't matter if you are at work or at home. When you ignore your own needs, stress or displeasure results. Some people internalize these feelings. Later these feelings come out as anger, rage, or physical symptoms like stomach pains and backaches. We waste too much time on control busters: feelings that zap our energy and steal our time. In this chapter you will learn about four control busters. They are:

1. *Fear*—how to feel fear and work to overcome it.

2. *Worry*—how to eliminate worry so we can enjoy today.

3. *Failure*—a temporary setback which teaches us valuable lessons.

4. *Adversity*—how opportunity comes from challenging times.

Ask yourself these two important questions: "Are you living the kind of life you want?", and, "Are you taking care of your needs as well as spending time with people who are important to you?" If you answer "no," please read on.

Remember, *The magic inside you is no hocus pocus. Set your goals and you create the focus.* All the answers to life's riddles are within your own heart. You already possess the answers to enable you to gain the control and enjoyment you deserve from life. Why not go full speed ahead with them?

I use the following exercise to open my workshops on stress management. I ask participants to gather into small groups and think of ways to show they are working too hard. Some of their comical answers follow. You are working too hard if:

- You rush home from your "9 to 5" job just in time to catch the 11 o'clock news.
- You wake up at 6 a.m. and dress for work before you realize it is your day off.
- You answer your home phone with your company name.
- You buy new underwear because you don't have time to do your laundry.
- Your dog doesn't recognize you.

With some clues to identify whether you are working too hard, let's discuss each of the four control busters that may be stopping you from living a more joyful life. Thousands of wonderful people I have spoken with over the years have shared with me how they sabotage themselves.

FEAR. We are born with only two fears, which may surprise you: the fear of falling and the fear of loud noises. We acquire all other fears. We put negative thoughts and messages into our own minds. Look at the word "fear" and think about this acronym:

F = false

E = evidence

A = appearing

R = real

So what can we do to face fear? My workshop participants tell me how they face fear and fight it. They admit it is not easy. But it is possible.

A woman in one of my workshops told me she was recently diagnosed with multiple sclerosis. She voiced her concerns to others in her support group. "What if I am forced to use a wheel chair? What if I cannot go on walks with my family on beautiful spring days?" The facilitator of the support group told the concerned woman that if anything was to cripple her, it would be her "what ifs." The truth is, she may never realize any of those fears.

We must silence the internal noise inside our minds. We have the power and control to lead calmer, stronger lives. We must force ourselves to eliminate fearful and destructive thoughts. Fear does not help tomorrow's troubles, and it surely ruins today's happiness. So what good is it?

When I tell people that I give one hundred workshops and speeches each year before thousands of people, the typical responses are, "I could never do that!" or "I would love to speak, but I am so afraid." Public speaking is a common fear many people experience. Other common fears include the fear of heights, financial problems, drowning, sickness, death, flying, loneliness, insects, and dogs.

There *are* ways to face fears and overcome them. Every time I speak to a new group I give myself a pep talk. I stand in front of a mirror in the hotel room and say, "Yes, Joyce, you can do it. Your message is important and the group needs to hear your words!" I stand up straight and do deep breathing exercises. Then, with renewed confidence, I go off to do the best I can to help others become driven by change, which will enable them to live richer lives.

I belong to the National Speakers Association. This incredible group, comprised of over 3,500 members, shares speaking techniques with other professional speakers, along with additional secrets for success. One of the most important things I have learned from my professional and supportive peers is that many speakers give themselves the same pep talk that I do. We feel the fear and use various techniques to overcome it.

Too many people give in to their fears, and then their dread consumes them. Fear really is *false evidence appearing real.* Watch babies crawl around and explore their new world. They examine things with curiosity and without fear. Step back and take a look at situations in your life which usually invoke fear. Then work hard to overcome them.

WORRY. The second control buster is worry. Look at the time we spend worrying about things that probably will never happen. Worry is mentally rehearsing a potential disaster. Ask yourself how you want to spend your time, worrying about "what ifs" or living a joyous life.

A scene in the movie *Grand Canyon* finds actor Danny Glover looking at the majestic gorge and contemplating his life, full of disappointments and worry. He says, "It is a real joke, my worries compared to the magnificent design of this place. It has been here for so long and will be in existence longer than any of my worries." Remember this scene the next time you allow worry to creep into your mind and consume your thoughts.

My favorite quote about worry is by American author and humorist Mark Twain. He said, "I've had a lot of trouble in my life, most of which never happened." Think about all the times you didn't want to go to a meeting or a party. You worried about who you would sit with or who would be there. Afterward, you probably realized how much you enjoyed yourself. The very things that gnawed at you never materialized.

We worry about yesterday and tomorrow. Yesterday has passed and so have our mistakes and blunders. We cannot erase a single word we said or act we did. Tomorrow can be a great day full of promise and excitement, or a sad day full of regrets and fear. We have a choice of how we live today. Think of this moment. None of us knows what tomorrow will bring and yesterday is history. Today is all that really matters.

How many times do we worry about things and ruin our present situation because we don't see the marvelous opportunities right in front of us. Worry does not help tomorrow's troubles, but it does ruin today's happiness. British Prime Minister Winston Churchill had important advice for us when he said, "Let your advance worrying become advance thinking and planning."

Remember, *we have choices* about our thoughts. We change television channels when we are bored or don't like the program. How about doing the same thing with your mind? Imagine a brilliant red sunset. Notice the sun disappearing into the horizon. Nothing is left except a gorgeous pink sky. Now switch your mental channel and see a pitch-black sky with a full moon beaming at you. Visualize two cows jumping over the moon. Switch your mental channel again. Now see a red fire engine and hear the sirens blasting. Picture yourself behind the wheel wearing the fire chief's hat.

Were you able to do this exercise? You can do the same thing with your mind. Just switch off the worry channel! It's not easy because worry becomes habit. Yet we can change any habit once we are *ready* to change.

FAILURE. The third control buster is failure. Failures are only temporary setbacks. We learn our most important lessons through failure. American automobile manufacturer Henry Ford said, "Failure is an opportunity to begin again more intelligently."

As a professional speaker I have learned a great deal from failure. I know that every audience will not jump to its feet with applause or run to me with compliments at the conclusion of every workshop. They may not laugh at every humorous story, or clap at every magic trick I use to prove a point. Sometimes people don't respond positively. Believe me, any performer—whether in sports, theater, or professional speaking—have those times in their careers when they are disillusioned and feel as though they want to quit. My message is: *learn* from these experiences. People who quit after failure miss life's important lessons. Former NFL and Green Bay Packer coach Vince Lombardi said, "It's not whether you get knocked down, it's whether you get up again."

Henry Ford also observed, "Obstacles are those frightful things you see when you take your eyes off your goal." Actress Tallulah Bankhead remarked, "If I had my life to live over again I'd make the same mistakes, only sooner." Chinese philosopher Lao-tzu declared, "Failure? No! Just temporary setbacks. To see things in the seed, that is genius." Then there was comedian W.C. Fields who quipped, "If at first you don't succeed, try, try again, then give up. There's no use being a damn fool about it."

The following people didn't listen to W.C. Field's message, but did listen to Winston Churchill who asserted, "Never, never, never, give up." The following are actual rejection notices received when these famous and incredibly successful books were first submitted for publication. George Orwell, the author of *Animal Farm*, was spurned by, "It is impossible to sell animal stories in the USA." A critic of *The Diary of Anne Frank* by Anne Frank, stated, "The girl doesn't have a special perception or feeling which would lift that book above the curiosity level." And *Lust for Life*, by Irving Stone, was described as, "A long, dull novel about an artist."

A workshop participant gave me the following article, *Don't Be Afraid To Fail.*

You've failed many times, although you may not remember. You fell down the first time you tried to walk. You almost drowned the first time you tried to swim, didn't you? Did you hit the ball the first time you swung a bat? Heavy hitters, the ones who hit the most home runs, also strike out a lot. R.H. Macy failed seven times before his department store in New York caught on. English novelist John Creasey got 753 rejections slips before he published 564 books. Babe Ruth struck out 1,330 times, but he also hit 714 home runs.

Don't worry about failure. Worry about the chances you miss when you don't even try.[2]

We dream about the perfect event, the perfect vacation, the perfect relationship, the perfect wedding, and the perfect job. But when we think about it, the stories we retell every year tend to be memories of imperfection: the time Mom dropped the cake, the time Junior broke his arm showing off, and the time Dad missed his surprise party. So the next time you find yourself reeling from some terrible failure, remember that someday you will look back on it and laugh. Then tell yourself, "If someday I am going to laugh about this, I might as well laugh about it now."

My mission is to plant seeds in the minds of my audiences. I am not responsible for reaping their harvest; that is up to them. They must decide what changes to make, and what chances to take. My commitment is to coach them to be their personal best.

Years ago, when I was getting ready for one of my first speeches on team building, I gave myself a pep talk. I was prepared to speak to an audience of 50 people. But the minute I began the program I knew I was in trouble. No one made an effort to move when given instructions to find a new partner. No one smiled when I told my signature story, one that always received a positive response. I was devastated. This was my first flop.

Afterward I talked to the meeting planner and found out that the audience had just come from a three-hour cocktail party. Some members wanted to continue partying, while others wanted to go to sleep. What they *didn't* want was to hear a program on team building.

I learned important lessons about my career that day: to take any failures in stride, to do extensive research for every speech or workshop, and to look at the agenda

---

[2]A message as published in the *Wall Street Journal* by ©United Technologies Corporation (1986). Reprinted with permission.

prior to my presentation. I learned to ask the program goals. I need to know as much about the audience as possible before I conduct a workshop. Today meeting planners and participants express their appreciation of my methods to learn all about their company or association. That one difficult speech years ago taught me the value of research. Most of all, it taught me never to give presentations after cocktail parties!

When we are experiencing down times in our lives, we must look really hard for the positives. They are there! When I came home from that devastating program there were flowers waiting for me. A note, in my husband's handwriting, said, "You may have bombed with that audience, but you are still dynamite with me!"

I always coach groups on the importance of making mistakes. Management expert Peter Drucker wrote, "The better a man is the more mistakes he will make, and the more new things he will try. I would never promote into a top level job a man who was not making mistakes, otherwise he is sure to be mediocre."

ADVERSITY. The fourth control buster is adversity. Life gives us an opportunity to look for positives in every negative situation. Finding the positive is a real test when we are down and out physically, financially, or emotionally. Yet something good usually comes from adversity.

Terry, a salesperson and workshop participant, shared with me how getting fired from her first job was the best thing that ever happened to her. She always told her prospects, "When you buy our product, I will show you a magic trick." People loved this and she was a high producer in her company. But Terry's boss didn't like her different, yet effective approach. He told her she didn't fit into the corporate mold and asked her to find employment elsewhere.

Terry was devastated at first. She was out of a job and felt like a failure. After some soul-searching, she decided to change her focus and teach other salespeople how to use "magic" when closing a deal. Now she is much more satisfied in her work, makes more money, loves her day, and her blood pressure is normal again. Remember, Terry saw no positives when dismissed, but she was persistent and pursued her dreams and goals.

A life-changing event for me began in 1989 when I was hired to speak in the Cayman Islands to a group of record store managers from the United States. My son, Ron, accompanied me to assist in the program. We became acquainted with this impressive group before the presentation and enjoyed the blue sky and perfect weather. Suddenly we learned a hurricane was fast approaching the island. The hotel personnel instructed us to quickly gather our valuables and board the busses which would take us to hurricane shelters. The Constable asked us to sign papers denoting next of kin. He said the island was flat and the waves could drown us if winds reached the expected 200 miles per hour. I allowed fear to take over. I started to panic. I felt guilty for bringing my son along. But Ron encouraged me to stop worrying because things could turn out all right after all. He reassured me by calmly saying words he had heard me use with my family and at workshops. I needed to be jolted into reality, and his words did the trick.

We heard the howling winds and the sound of uprooted trees crashing to the ground. The roof of another shelter caved in and 200 more people joined us in our already crowded quarters. We heard the death count from the storm in Jamaica on the radio. People were concerned about their loved ones on other islands. Some were screaming, others were getting drunk. Ron and I started talking to total strangers about how we would change our lives if we survived. Fortunately, the eye of the hurricane missed us by 20 miles.

Near tragedy taught me much about myself and my life than I ever knew before the hurricane. First, you have to be flexible, like the oak tree and the reed in Aesop's fable. You never know when "hurricanes" will come into your life. Second, it doesn't matter who you are or where you come from, we have inner resources that make us strong. The magic is not how well you do overall, but how well you deal with the stress in your life. How you handle adversity is more important than how well you handle success. Third, when you face death, you value life even more. Every single day is precious; run away from people who complain and moan about trivial things. Fourth, I was reminded about my important value system—my family and my career, in that order.

My priorities were in the wrong order before Hurricane Gilbert blew into my life. I was putting more energy into my career than my family. I was on a treadmill and didn't even realize it. Now I see how my family helps to keep me going. They are my coaches, cheering me on when I get an exciting speaking engagement, and gently kicking me in the seat of the pants when I need it. I learned never to take them for granted.

You may not face death or hurricanes each day but you do face obstacles. Ask yourself how you would react if a storm hit your life. How much do you appreciate what you have now? Do you value your loved ones, your health, your job? In 1933 Will Rogers said, "Nothing makes a person more broad-minded like adversity."

All four of the control busters—fear, worry, failure, and adversity—await you every day. You must realize how strong you are. You need to change your mental channels when fear and worry come into your mind. You need to see failures as learning experiences and stepping stones to success. You need to look within and find inner strength when adversity strikes in order to go full speed ahead.

At the end of your day stop and look at what went right. If you knew you'd be struck by lightning in six months, what would you do differently today? Roman philosopher Marcus Aurelius wrote, "Execute every act of life as though it were thy last." And comedian Joe E.

Lewis maintained, "You only live once, but if you work it right, once is enough."

Are You Burned Out?

Determine whether you are prone to burnout by taking a few moments to respond to this quiz. Give yourself ten points for every "yes" answer.

	Yes	No
1. Do you consider yourself a perfectionist?	__	__
2. Do you find it difficult to say "no"?	__	__
3. Do you frequently skip meals because you are too busy to eat?	__	__
4. Do you never have enough time to do what you want?	__	__
5. Do you find it difficult to delegate authority?	__	__
6. Do you feel guilty about your inability to do everything?	__	__
7. Do you handle chores and situations as they arise rather than planning ahead?	__	__
8. Do you rarely relax, exercise, have fun, or do something beneficial for yourself?	__	__
9. Do you feel you have no control over your situation?	__	__
10. Are you always catering to the needs of others?	__	__

Now check your score:

0–20	Under control
30–40	Super-person characteristics
50–60	Borderline super-person
70–100	Full-fledged super-person

Action Plan
Chapter 2

BATTERY

Stress: Re-charge Your Battery by Channeling Stress into Positive Energy

When you discover new ideas, or ways of performing a task better, write them down. It has been found that if new ideas aren't used within 24 hours, they are generally forgotten. Make a copy of this plan and place it in a prominent location in your home or office. Make sure you try all of the things you have made note of.

1._____

2._____

3._____

4._____

5._____

Top performers are people who realize they have to take care of themselves first, mentally and physically. They are in control of their own lives even during stressful times. They take their lives seriously and themselves lightly. How do you take care of your own needs during stressful times?

_____

_____

_____

_____

Chapter 3

Humor: Use High-octane Humor

Each day more and more people see the value of humor in improving their lives. We are buying more personal growth books and tapes on the topic of fulfillment than ever before. Many people want to know:

- How can I lighten up?
- How do I deal with the pressures in today's stressful world?
- How can I feel more relaxed at home?
- How can I bring excitement back to personal relationships?
- How can I make work more enjoyable?
- How can I become closer to family members?

In this chapter, you will learn how to add more fun to your daily life and bring out the humor that already exists.

You may be saying, "I'm not a funny person. I can't tell a joke. My life is full of pressure and nothing enjoyable or funny ever happens to me." Believe it or not, you *do* have the ability to enjoy more upbeat days, at home and at work. The answers lie within.

The seven main themes in this chapter are:

1. The importance of humor.
2. The difference between childlike and childish behavior.
3. How to have fun.
4. How to take yourself lightly and your life seriously.
5. How to develop a sense of joy in your life.
6. How corporations and government agencies use humor to increase productivity.
7. Exciting ideas to get you started.

I ask my workshop participants to brainstorm the question: "How can you guarantee yourself a life that is totally serious and dull?" At first they look confused, then they begin to have fun with the question. They answer:

- Don't play with children.
- Don't read the comics.
- Don't watch sitcoms on television.
- Concentrate on the sad times in life.
- Never cheer up a person who needs encouragement.
- Take yourself very seriously and condemn yourself when you make a mistake.
- Don't laugh for fear someone may think you are silly and childish.
- Don't smile because smiles give you wrinkles.

Successful television programs and newspaper columns reflect what people *want* and *need*, that is, laughter and humor. The most popular sitcoms in the past have been *I Love Lucy*, *The Jack Benny Show*, *Taxi*, *The Cosby Show*, *Roseanne*, *Seinfeld*, *Grace Under Fire*, and *Frasier*. The most celebrated of the syndicated columnists include humorists Erma Bombeck, Art Buchwald, and Dave Barry.

The greeting card industry is wildly successful with its comical and witty cards. Humor in advertising is refreshing, provides stress relief, and sells more products and services. Look in the humor section of a bookstore, you may be amazed how this department has grown. People need escape from their pressurized world. We want to laugh; it's healthy. Of course, humor is not for everyone. It is only for people who want to feel pleasure, be alive, and enjoy life.

Most people cannot tell a joke effectively. Those who do have lucrative careers—thanks to good material, expert timing, delivery, pizzazz, guts, and talent. Most of us groan when our friends tell a joke and stumble over the punch line. I realize I am not necessarily funny, yet I am fun to be with. Think about that statement for a moment. And think about people you like to be around. Are they funny, or fun to be with?

By now, you may wonder how this book can help you lighten up. Read on.

"Some day I will laugh at this," is a statement most everyone makes at least once in their life. Well, learn not to wait for some day. If you are going to look back on something years later and laugh, why wait?

People say, "I will have fun. But not now, I'm much too busy. I'll have fun on vacation or on my day off." Don't postpone joy and laughter. You never know what tomorrow will bring. How sad it is to see people waste their precious today.

Some of my favorite quotes are:

- Comedian Lily Tomlin, as her Edith Ann character said, "When I'm happy, I feel like crying, but when I'm sad, I don't feel like laughing. I think it's better to be happy. Then you get two feelings for the price of one."

- "The really happy person is one who can enjoy the scenery on a detour." —Anonymous

- Actress Mae West said, "Too much of a good thing is wonderful!"

- Comedian George Burns quipped, "If I get big laughs, I'm a comedian. If I get little laughs, I'm a humorist. If I get no laughs, I'm a singer."

- Greek philosopher Plato stated, "Life should be lived as a play."

- Statesman Ben Franklin said, "The Constitution only guarantees the American people the right to pursue happiness. You have to catch it yourself."

- Another great observation is, "Happiness consists of living each day as if it were the first day of your honeymoon and the last day of your vacation."

- Comedian Bob Hope, at age 91, was asked why he hadn't retired—since he could easily afford to—and gone fishing. Hope replied, "Because fish don't laugh and applaud."

People are surprised to learn that humor helps develop a set of skills and an outlook on life which assists them in their work and in their everyday life. Here are four key reasons why humor is so important:

1. Humor increases productivity at work.
2. You stay healthier when you laugh.
3. Laughter releases stress when you are in crisis.
4. Humor helps you thrive in the face of change.

During challenging times, humor relieves tension and keeps us flexible and fluid—not rigid and breakable. As water brings life to any environment, humor nurtures life and makes it worth the effort. Successful corporations are discovering that people work more effectively and productively when humor is part of their workday.

Research shows that when people play more enthusiastically they stay healthier. The French physician Voltaire wrote in 1770, "The art of medicine consists of amusing the patient while nature cures the disease." English satirist Jonathan Swift wrote, "The best doctors in the world are Dr. Diet, Dr. Quiet, and Dr. Merryman." Humor is serious business because it helps us remain creative while under pressure. Brainstorming sessions tumble along like white water and new ideas pour out when people laugh.

Humor helps us thrive in the midst of constant change. Some people are defeated, not by change, but by their own rigidity. A young father told his son, "Things were so difficult when I was your age. I actually had to get up off the couch and walk cross the room to change the TV channels." Think about changes in your life since you were a child. It's quite amazing.

The value of humor is best reflected in a crisis. When I was in graduate school, I thought it was inappropriate when a professor asked comedians to speak at a class on death and dying. Mothers and fathers of deceased children shared their grieving process with us. But, to my surprise, the parents related how humor helped them get through their pain.

After the death of my wonderful father, Joseph, I also learned how humor could help me cope through the grieving process. Instead of concentrating on his last few months in a hospital bed, I reminded myself of all the happy times I had with him. I smile when I recall his reaction to my newly dyed orange hair when I was 15 years old. To those who have teenagers, remember that the times that drive you crazy now will make you laugh sometime in the future. So why not laugh now?

I have come to realize the necessity of humor in my training sessions also. When I discuss serious issues like prejudice, anger, communication, conflict, control, and fear, I add an element of fun so the pressure does not become too burdensome. A few years ago I added magical illusions to my workshops. People tell me they enjoy the magic and ask for more. They love the release of energy and the element of fun it injects into each session. The tricks and levity reinforce a rule I live by—take yourself lightly and your life seriously.

I remember an incident that happened when Ron, my son, was moving from our home to his first apartment. He decided to be creative and throw his mattress from the upstairs loft down to the first floor. In the process, he destroyed my favorite piece of crystal. He felt horrible when he heard the glass crash to the floor. And I saw the look of panic on his face. My first reaction was to yell and scream and to tell him that his actions were reckless and irresponsible. Instead I gritted my teeth, bit my tongue, and said, "Crystal can be replaced. It is more important for you to never repeat that brilliant move again." As a humor and self-esteem coach I had to remind myself to practice what I preach.

My reaction fit with my value system. Why should I make him feel worse than he already felt? Ron laughs today at how my words sounded so right and so nonjudgmental—while my clenched jaw showed him that I really wanted to strangle him. I asked myself how important this broken glass would be two years from now versus his self-esteem. He thanks me today. Ron is married now, and one day when he is a father, I am confident he will do the same thing for his child.

British novelist H. G. Wells said, "The crisis of today is the joke of tomorrow." And many people remember Will Rogers' well known statement, "I don't make jokes. I watch the government and report the facts."

Did you know every United States president since Franklin D. Roosevelt has had a gag writer on his team? President Harry Truman mused, "Any man who has had the job I've had and didn't possess a sense of humor wouldn't still be here."

Comedian Jimmy Durante said, "It dawned on me that as long as I could laugh, I was safe from the world; and I have learned since, that laughter keeps me safe from myself, too. All of us have schnozes that are ridiculous in one way or another, if not in our faces, then in our characters, minds or habits. When we admit our schnozes, instead of defending them, we begin to laugh, and the world laughs with us."

To quote Will Rogers again, "Everything is funny as long as it is happening to someone else." People who can laugh at themselves can relate better to others by showing their vulnerabilities. They will never cease to be amused. I notice that people have more eye contact with me when I tell of my own blunders. We love to hear others share stories about their mistakes.

The following may sound rather clinical, like a disease or an affliction, but it is really a description of a person laughing. The body temperature rises a degree, and the pulse rate and blood pressure increase. The muscles contract, the vocal chords quiver, and the face contorts. Pressure builds in the lungs. The lower jaw suddenly becomes uncontrollable, and breath expels from the mouth at nearly 70 miles per hour.

Do you know how important smiling and laughter are to all of us? It takes seventeen muscles to smile and forty-three muscles to frown. One of my favorite sayings is, "Keep smiling. It makes people wonder what you've been up to."

The *American Heritage Dictionary Of The English Language* defines laughing in this way: "To express certain emotions, especially mirth, delight, or derision, by a series of spontaneous, usually unarticulated sounds often accompanied by corresponding facial and bodily movements."[3]

Are you familiar with endorphins? They are chemicals produced in the brain. Their structure almost matches synthetic morphine. They can deliver pain relief similar to medications. They elevate the "inner uppers," a phrase coined by Dr. Dale Anderson, that raise our spirits and lift our moods. Thirty-seven endorphins are released by laughing, satisfying relationships, setting and reaching goals, enjoying parties, exercising regularly, and soaking up nature. Think about the last time you had a really good belly laugh. Was it a natural high? Your endorphins were flowing.

Here are some great expressions on laughter. A Yiddish proverb states, "What soap is to the body, laughter is to the soul." And comedian Milton Berle said, "Laughter is an instant vacation." Mark Twain remarked, "The human race has only one really effective weapon and that is laughter." Actor Alan Alda mused, "When people are laughing, they're generally not killing one another." Author Norman Cousins reported, "Laughter is a form of internal jogging. Ten minutes of genuine belly laughter has an anesthetic effect and will give me at least two hours of pain free sleep." Comedian Victor Borge quipped, "Laughter is the shortest distance between two people."

Some people have a problem distinguishing between childish and childlike behavior. Childish qualities are selfishness, infantile behavior, whining, pouting, and throwing tantrums—not the best qualities to have. On the other hand, childlike people are curious, open, spontaneous, flexible, creative, playful, and joyful.

When workshop participants divide into groups to problem-solve they display positive childlike behavior. The noise level increases when I ask them to rediscover and discuss their favorite childhood games and songs. It is refreshing to hear their joyous laughter. Every time people act childlike in a workshop something positive comes from the experience. Think about your favorite game, playmate, or toys when you were a child. I can picture a smile coming to your face.

Some cynical or straight-laced adults think people who laugh are airheads and don't take life seriously. Too bad they don't see the importance that humor plays in our lives. American poet Robert Frost wrote, "Forgive my nonsense as I also forgive the nonsense of those who think they talk sense." It is hard for some people to become childlike because they hear messages from their past saying, "Wipe that smile off your face!" or "Wait until you have kids!" Again, people need to take themselves lightly and their world seriously. Movie critic Gene Shalit said, "Being funny doesn't mean you aren't serious." The old English word for silly means to be happy or prosperous. Are you starting to see the value of childlike, innocent behavior?

Halloween was a holiday I loved to celebrate when my children were young. We decorated the house with ghosts and goblins. I dressed in costumes when I accompanied them "trick or treating." One Halloween I dressed as a tree. We had an unforgettable time. One "sophisticated" neighbor asked my daughter, Wendy, why I would want to do such a thing! The neighbor didn't have a clue.

My audiences learn more from my workshops if they see that I am having a good time. Fun is contagious. I come by this childlike quality honestly. My mother, Sara, is the kind of person others love to be around. She has a positive outlook, an engaging smile, and is fun to be with. I love the expression, "We are only young once, but with humor, we can be immature forever." Another favorite is, "We don't stop playing because we grow old; we grow old because we stop playing."

British novelist Agatha Christie describes the process of a woman aging in a positive way. She quipped, "An archaeologist is the best husband any woman could have. The older she gets, the more he is interested."

Author C. W. Metcalf writes about Sylvie in his book *Lighten Up: Survival Skills For People Under Pressure.* One day Sylvie was walking with her husband and one of his younger friends, Herbert, who was in his eighties. They stopped at a corner and Sylvie started to dance a jig. She loved to dance. She would rather dance than stand still. Her husband, accustomed to this behavior, took no notice. But Herbert said, "For goodness sake, Sylvie, act your age." Sylvie replied to Herbert, "You better be careful Herbert, I've buried everyone who ever told me that."[4]

Illusionist David Copperfield ends his incredible show with this message, "Never give up your childlike sense of wonder and joy. Nothing is as important as keeping the magic alive."

---

[4]*LIGHTEN UP: SURVIVAL SKILLS FOR PEOPLE UNDER PRESSURE* (pp 41, 132-133), © 1992 by C.W. Metcalf & Roma Felible. Reprinted with permission of Addison-Wesley Publishing Company, Inc.

Work Sheet
Chapter 3

Fun Activities

Plan a fun activity every day for a month. Keep a record of your experiences and notice the positive effects on the quality of your life.

	Week 1	Week 2	Week 3	Week 4
Sun				
Mon				
Tues				
Wed				
Thurs				
Fri				
Sat				

Action Plan
Chapter 3

Humor: Use High-octane Humor

When you discover new ideas, or ways of performing a task better, write them down. It has been found that if new ideas aren't used within 24 hours, they are generally forgotten. Make a copy of this plan and place it in a prominent location in your home or office. Make sure you try all of the things you have made note of.

1._____

2._____

3._____

4._____

5._____

Top performers are people who are responsible for their own morale. They do not let negativity drain away their energy. They realize they are coaches for themselves and others. How they act at home or at work sets the tone for those around them. What can you do today to increase your own morale?

_____

_____

_____

_____

_____

_____

Chapter 4

Having Fun:
Tune Up Your Funny Bone

Now that we have reassurance that it is okay to act childlike at times, let's discover how to have fun. Workshop participants say to me, "I like this workshop. I like the way it makes me feel. But you don't know me, my family, or my job. There is never anything funny happening to me. Tell me how I can regain fun in my everyday life."

Having fun will be a challenge for those of you who share these feelings. Fun and humor can and do exist in your life; they are everywhere. Comedian Mel Brooks said, "Life literally abounds in comedy if you just look around you."

Start with this exercise. Look around you for red items. You'll see red in clothes, food, rugs, furniture, buildings, signs, nature, hair, cosmetics, and toys. The same principle applies when we search for humor and fun. It may take time, but once you are attuned to looking for humor, you will easily find it.

Every time I perform a magical illusion in my workshops, something humorous happens. I once asked a volunteer to help an imaginary friend select a color for a new car. I then asked the volunteer what color was chosen. The answer was supposed to end the illusion. But instead the volunteer started giving a long speech on how she couldn't make a decision for a friend because that would not teach self-responsibility. She went on and on with her explanation. The audience started laughing, thinking the volunteer was part of the magic trick. I am definitely more careful when selecting an assistant now. But if the illusion does not work out as anticipated, I can always find humor in some aspect of the experience.

Writer Nathaniel Hawthorne said, "Happiness is a butterfly, which, when pursued, is always just beyond your grasp. But if you sit down quietly, it may settle on you." Remember Helen Keller, the American memoirist and lecturer, who learned to speak although she was born deaf and blind? Her words make a lot of sense to me: "When one door of happiness closes, another opens, but often we look so long at the closed door that we don't see the one that has been opened for us."

People inject humor into their daily lives in countless ways. A doctor in New York had a 22-year-old son and a 26-year-old daughter. He set up his answering machine message to respond to his grown children. He taped this message: "If you are in an emotional turmoil over a breakup with a romantic partner and require a few hours of sympathetic discussion, press one. If you require financial assistance, press two. If you are being treated unfairly at work or school and wish to displace your anger to a nuclear family member, press three. If your car or household appliances need immediate repair or replacement, press four. If you are telephoning to inquire about our well being or to pass a few moments of pleasant topical conversation, please check the number you intended to dial."

A friend's 12-year-old son brought home 4 D's and 3 F's on his report card. The boy asked his father, "What do you think my problem is, heredity or environment?"

One of my favorite comic strip characters, capturing mother-daughter relationships, is *Cathy*. Cathy says, "I love you Mom, but I'll never be like you. I'll never think like you. I'll never act like you. I'll never look like you." Cathy's Mom replied, "Oh, I know. I used to say the exact same thing to my mother, and I wound up thinking just like her, acting just like her, looking like her. See, you're just like me already." Cathy runs from the room screaming, and Mom says, "Oh, isn't that cute, that's just what I used to do."[5] Look at your relationships and see what kind of cartoon captions you could write.

A classic scene from the TV show *Cheers* had Carla, the barmaid, and Norm, the customer, talking about failure. Norm said, "Carla, I've always had a fear of failure." Carla responded, "Norm, you *are* a failure." Norm smiled and remarked, "Then I've licked it!"

An incident was featured on television and in the newspapers. A crazed man with an automatic weapon boarded a crowded New York commuter train and started shooting randomly. Several people were injured or killed. A father and son—who worked together, rode the train together each day, and enjoyed a close relationship—were both victims. The father was killed and the son, an only child, was severely wounded, brain damaged and paralyzed on one side. The wife/mother of the two victims was devastated. She stayed by her son's side at the hospital each day until it was time to bury her husband. She had not yet told her son of his father's death. When she returned from the funeral her son asked where she had been all day. His father's death was devastating news, and the mother

---

[5]Cathy Guisewite © used by permission of Universal Press Syndicate.

could see a setback in her son's recovery. But she clung to his side and offered support and encouragement.

One day the mother sensed her son was depressed so she gave him a pep talk about courage and perseverance. The son looked at his mom and said, "I want to be handicapped." The mother was desperate. "Why?" she asked. The son looked his mother in the eyes and replied, "Better parking!" From that moment she knew he was still a fighter and that everything would be fine. In spite of this horrendous tragedy, he had maintained his sense of humor.

Anyone who has ever flown on an airplane has a humorous story regarding a late arrival, lost luggage, or unappetizing food. Instead of concentrating on the negative part of travel, start looking for the funny episodes. I have earned the right to speak on this subject because I often fly on business trips.

One of my recent flights was delayed for over an hour. The passengers were in and out of their seats and many were grumbling. As takeoff time approached, the pilot said, "Ladies and Gentlemen, will you please clear the aisles and take your seats so I can see out of the rear view mirror." As the plane taxied onto the runway, he made a few more humorous remarks, easing the tension so the passengers were relaxed and in better moods.

Another pilot explained why the airplane was in a holding pattern. "We're experiencing a slight delay but it is nothing to worry about. They're turning the airport around, and we're going to wait up here until they get it just right for us." The passengers smiled and relaxed.

Steve Allen Jr., a medical doctor and son of comedian Steve Allen, travels the world teaching people how to relieve stress by juggling. Dr. Allen was on a flight when suddenly the attendant started crawling on the floor of the plane screaming, "Where is it? Where is it?" Steve Jr. hunched down to the floor and asked, "What are you looking for?" She answered with a big smile, "Where is the glamour they promised me in this job?" Everyone on the plane started to laugh. These little vignettes show us that we can find humor in almost every situation. We can concentrate on the negatives, or we can look past them and find the things that are comical in our lives.

Now that we've discussed where to find humor, let's concentrate on learning how to lighten up, which most people want and need to learn. Yes, our lives are serious. Yes, the workforce is competitive. And, yes, we create a lot of pressure for ourselves. For all these reasons we need to take our lives seriously and ourselves lighter. Abraham Lincoln remarked, "Most folks are about as happy as they make up their minds to be."

C. W. Metcalf tells another story, this one about Chuck, a brave little boy who was dying. Chuck said, "I want to give this list to my Mom and Dad after I die. It's a list of all the fun we had, all the times we laughed. Like the time Mom and Dad and Chrissie and Linda and me dressed like those guys in the Fruit Of The Loom™ underwear commercial. Dad was driving us to a costume party when the police stopped our car for speeding. Dad was dressed like a bunch of grapes and I was an apple, and the others were different things like bananas and stuff. When the policewoman came up to the car she looked in and started laughing really hard. I mean, she could hardly stand up. We all started laughing with the police officer. Then she said, 'Where are you all headed, a salad bar?' Dad said he was sorry to be speeding, but his kids were getting ripe and they were starting to draw flies. The officer laughed so hard that she had to take off her dark glasses and wipe tears from her eyes. She finally said, 'Well, get out of here, but go slow! I don't want to find you squashed all over the highway.'"

Chuck also had a letter ready for his parents that read, "I know you are real upset right now that I'm going away, but I don't want you to forget this stuff.

I don't want you to remember me as being skinny and sick. I want you to think about the good times we had, because that is what I remember most."[6]

When I am around people who concentrate on negative things, I do what I can to tell them they are wasting their today. If only the negative people of the world could meet a person like Chuck, maybe they would begin to look at the positives in their lives.

The next time you need to lighten up about a stressful situation, do the following exercise. Close your eyes and draw your conflict with the *opposite* hand that you would normally use. This brings an automatic laugh. Somehow your conflict does not look so serious anymore. People begin to overcome their problems at the moment they start laughing about them. Mark Twain wrote, "Humor is tragedy plus time."

We've looked at some ideas about how to lighten up, and I would like to share with you the importance of developing a sense of joy about life. I ask workshop participants to finish the following statement: For me to be more humorous, I am waiting for _____. A few samples of their funny lines are:

- Permission.
- The coffee to be ready.
- The barking dog next door to leave town.
- A better time.
- My youth to return.
- A better circle of friends.
- Spring.
- You to go first.

---

[6]*LIGHTEN UP: SURVIVAL SKILLS FOR PEOPLE UNDER PRESSURE* (pp 41, 132-133), © 1992 by C. W. Metcalf & Roma Felible. Reprinted by permission of Addison-Wesley Publishing Company, Inc.

When you find yourself taking life too seriously, consider these activities which should help you to lighten up:

1. Hang a big picture of your dream vacation on the wall and look at it when you need to escape.

2. Learn to juggle. Start with scarves, then move on to small objects. It is fun and a great way to relieve stress. For those who would like to learn more about this great stress reliever, contact the International Juggler's Association in Montague, Massachusetts.

3. Lock your desk drawer before you leave the office and yell "Stay!"

Many other activities can help you to lighten up also. Think about people you enjoy. Make a list, call them and make plans. Then go and have fun. You will make them feel great and you'll add a new dimension of fun to your life. My high school reunion committee had such fun planning a recent reunion that we decided to get together once a month thereafter. Even though most of us were not close friends in high school, we have a wonderful time together now. We all made new friends with different and interesting people.

Knowing you had only two weeks to live, how would you spend the time? Think about the things you love doing. What changes would you make? Remember, don't postpone joy. Work on adding joy and fun to your life today.

The following article, *If I Had My Life To Live Over*, was written by Nadine Stair at the age of 85:

If I had my life to live over, I'd try to make more mistakes next time. I would relax. I would limber up. I would be sillier than I have been this trip. I know of very few things I would take seriously.

I would be crazier. I would take more chances. I would take more trips. I would climb more mountains, swim more rivers and watch more sunsets. I would have more actual problems and fewer imaginary ones. You see, I am one of those people who lives sensibly and sanely, hour after hour, day after day. Oh, I have had my moments, and if I had it to do over again, I'd have more of them. In fact I'd have nothing else. Just moments, one after another, instead of living so many years ahead of each day. I have been one of those people who never goes anywhere without a thermometer, a hot water bottle, a gargle, a raincoat, and a parachute. If I had it to do over again, I would go places and do things and travel lighter than I have. If I had my life to live over, I would walk barefoot earlier in the Spring and stay that way later in the Fall. I would play hooky more. I would ride on more merry-go-rounds. I'd pick more daisies.[7]

Much of Nadine Stair's advice applies to all of us.

I find it intriguing to work with corporations, government agencies, and professional associations. I see wonderful programs they create to raise worker productivity by incorporating fun and humor into the workplace. They see that employees who have fun at work are less likely to be late or absent, and are apt to be more productive. The CEO of a huge corporation has a poster on her office door: "Notice! This office requires no physical fitness program. Everyone gets plenty of exercise jumping to conclusions, flying off the handle, running down the boss, knifing coworkers

---

[7] *If I Had To Live My Life Over* by Nadine Stair. This poem, which has been passed around and reprinted for years, has been attributed to Nadine Stair. It was supposedly written by her at age 85. The general consensus is that she was living in the state of Kentucky at the time she wrote the poem. We have been unable to contact any family to verify these claims.

in the back, dodging responsibility, polishing the apple and pushing their luck." What a great message to her employees to lighten up. And the president of a financial institution notes, "Don't look at me as a boss, but as a friend who is always right."

The following are some fascinating fun ideas from successful corporations:

- Ben and Jerry's Ice Cream—The company expects its employees to have a great day. If it's not fun, why do it? A "joy gang" improves the quality of life for employees and the community. It is a committee which asks what employees need to have in order to improve the atmosphere at work. In addition, each employee must take three pints of ice cream home daily.

- Southwest Airlines—Flight attendants are recruited for their sense of humor. They wear Halloween costumes and sing their safety regulations in rap. I've seen the flight attendants in action and they are very funny.

- A California dentist took his staff on a field trip to a shopping mall and gave each employee $200. He stipulated that they must buy at least five things and any money left after the two-hour shopping spree would be returned to him. At the next staff meeting, the employees had a "show and tell" session with their purchases. Can you imagine the stories and excitement!

- Pitney Bowes Corporation, based in Stafford, Connecticut, offers its employees courses in real estate, golf, tailoring, cake decorating, watercolor painting and photography. What fun!

- Bank of America in San Francisco has a "laugh-a-day" challenge for one month. Each employee tries to make coworkers laugh each day with cartoons and jokes. Winners receive T-shirts and books containing the best jokes and cartoons.

- The Walt Disney Company opens Disneyland to employees and their families exclusively for one night. Concessions and rides are run by upper management dressed in costume. Besides being a lot of fun, this event allows employees to see the theme park from the customer's perspective.

The list goes on and on. One of my clients covers employees' desks with balloons on their birthday. Ford Motor Company and AT&T use their own employees in commercials. Management guru and author Tom Peters says, "The number one premise of business is that it need not be boring or dull. It ought to be fun. If it is not fun, you're wasting your life." Many businesses are implementing ingenious ways of helping employees have fun.

Author and forecaster of business trends, John Naisbitt, states, "There is a new ideal about work emerging in America today. For the first time, there is a widespread expectation that work should be fulfilling and fun. For millions of baby boomers, this new ideal is not outrageous; it is natural." An upbeat working environment is much more productive than a routine environment. People who enjoy their work will come up with more ideas. Fun is contagious.

Fun ideas to get you started include theme days, such as Elvis impersonations, grungy or clashing clothes days, casual Fridays, talent contests, slogan contests, baby picture bulletin boards, wearing toy noses to meetings, toy car races, and, meeting team members at the airport gate in costume. You might create your own "joy gang" to find out what employees need to add more fun to their workday. Your list can be never-ending. These ideas will help you make your workday more enjoyable. When you find something you genuinely like to do—and make fun, joy, and creativity a part of your daily routine—you will never have to "work" another day in your life.

Remember the importance of humor. Concentrate on your childlike qualities; you were a kid once. The idea is to rekindle the child in you. Find magical and humorous moments in everything you do. Just open your eyes. You may want to keep a journal to record your findings. Don't waste too much time mentally beating yourself up . . . so you can go full speed ahead! Learn to take yourself lightly—the real key to finding a happier life. Ask yourself how important the crisis you are experiencing today will be in two years.

You don't have to tell a joke to be funny. Remember the good times and don't dwell on the sad memories. Ralph Waldo Emerson wrote, "To laugh often and much; to win respect of intelligent people and the affection of children; to leave the world a better place; to know even one life has breathed easier because you have lived. This is to have succeeded."

Actress Shirley MacLaine declares, "I think of life itself now as a wonderful play that I've written for myself. And so my purpose is to have the utmost fun playing my part."

Action Plan
Chapter 4

Having Fun:
Tune Up your Funny Bone

When you discover new ideas, or ways of performing a task better, write them down. It has been found that if new ideas aren't used within 24 hours, they are generally forgotten. Make a copy of this plan and place it in a prominent location in your home or office. Make sure you try all of the things you have made note of.

1._____

2._____

3._____

4._____

5._____

Chapter 5

Communication: It's a Two-way Street to Build Rapport

The ability to communicate is a basic need of the human race. Let's look at infants again. From the time babies learn to cry, they begin to use their voices as verbal tools; crying summons food and attention. This is communication at its most simple level. As we grow, communication seems to get more complex and confusing. Yet effective communicators take a tip from infants. They ask for what they want in a direct, clear, and concise way.

Communication problems are evident in the following concerns. Do any of the following comments sound like you?

- People don't take me seriously.
- People ignore me as if I'm invisible.
- I'm tired of people walking all over me.
- I'm too strong and seem to take over; I overwhelm others.

- I'm fed up because I make all the decisions. I want others to take a stand.

- People misunderstand my message.

- I'm afraid to make a presentation.

- How can I start a conversation?

- I don't like to meet new people; I find social gatherings very difficult.

It is easy to spot patterns here. People, from all walks of life, share the desire to communicate so others will listen and understand what they mean.

When was the last time poor communication caused you to lose money or feel embarrassed? The following anecdotes are from newspaper advertisements and articles. Read them and decide whether the intended message is being heard:

- Lost, one small apricot poodle. Neutered. Like one of the family.

- Dinner Special—Turkey $2.95; Chicken or Beef $2.25; Children $2.

- We don't tear your clothing with machines. We do it carefully by hand.

- Wonderful bargains for men with 15 and 17 necks.

- German Shepherd, easy to handle, loves to eat anything, especially children.

- Persons are prohibited from picking flowers from any but their own graves.

- My son is under the doctor's care and should not take physical education today. Please execute him.

These examples show that what we say matters. We must take great care to say what we mean!

Conversely, we must be careful when we accept communication from others. Our office gets at least one call a week from people looking for "speakers" in the Yellow Pages. They ask, "Do you sell stereo equipment?" They want home or automobile speakers, not a professional speaker. Quite a difference.

The core of communication is *what* you say and how others *hear* it. The following are examples of expressions Americans use as jargon:

- It's as clear as mud.
- The buck stops here.
- Down the drain.
- Ballpark figure.
- It won't fly.
- Raining cats and dogs.
- Don't make waves.

Obviously our meaning is not always crystal-clear. Just think how difficult it must be for people learning English as a second language to comprehend what we say.

Here are four important skills which will help you communicate better, thereby improving all areas of your life:

1. *Active Listening*. Hints to help you better understand what others are saying.

2. *Body Language and Nonverbal Communication*. How others read your mannerisms and actions.

3. *Networking Strategies*. Ideas to help you meet the kinds of people who can help you in your professional and personal life.

4. *Presentation Skills*. Learn how to look, sound, and feel confident in front of audiences and in one-on-one situations.

Active Listening

Greek philosopher Epictetus wrote, "Nature gave us one tongue and two ears so we could hear twice as much as we speak." Two statements I hear frequently are, "Listen, opportunity sometimes knocks very softly," and, "If you want me to be a good listener, give me something good to listen to." If all people were excellent communicators, it would be easier to listen. Improve your own style so you are available when you meet someone who needs help in listening.

What irritates you about the way others listen? Talking too much and interrupting are common complaints. Mark Twain said, "There is nothing so annoying as to have two people go right on talking when you are interrupting." Other annoying habits might be: avoiding eye contact, not smiling, fidgeting, tapping fingers, asking dumb questions about what was just said, putting words in the other person's mouth, and arguing. Think about what other people do that drives you crazy and the list will grow.

I constantly work to avoid jumping to conclusions. I have gotten into real trouble when I form an opinion before the other person finishes his or her message. Here's a letter from a daughter to her parents. This often told story is from an unknown source.

Dear Mom and Dad:

I'm sorry for not writing, but hope you will understand. First, sit down before you read further. I'm doing much better now after recovering from the broken leg I received jumping from the window when my apartment caught fire last month. I can almost walk normally again thanks to the loving care of Tom, the janitor who pulled me from the flames. He more than saved me; he's become my whole life. I have been living with him since the fire. We are planning on getting married. We haven't set a date yet, but will do so shortly, before my pregnancy shows. Yes, I'm pregnant. I knew you would be excited for me, knowing how much you want to be grandparents.

Your loving daughter,
Gail

P.S. There was no fire. My leg is not broken. I'm not pregnant, and there is no Tom. However I'm getting an "F" in Biology and wanted you to see that grade in its proper perspective.

I love the following classic story which shows the importance of not making assumptions.

An 80-year-old man went to his doctor for a checkup. The doctor told him, "You are in terrific shape. There's nothing wrong with you. Why, you might live forever. By the way, how old was your father when he died?" The patient responded, "Did I say he was dead?" The doctor was astonished. "You mean to tell me you are 80-years-old and your father is still alive?" "Not only that," said the patient, "my grandfather is 126 years old, and next week he's getting married." "Why on earth does your grandfather want to get married?" asked the doctor. The patient looked at the doctor and said, "Did I say he *wanted* to?"

Ralph Waldo Emerson wrote, "It's a luxury to be understood." The next time you're actively listening, notice if you are showing interest in the conversation. Are you asking relevant questions that show you're interested? Or are you waiting to tell *your* story?

I give workshop participants an interesting, yet difficult, exercise. I ask one person to talk to another about a complex situation or conflict they are experiencing. The listener cannot give advice, only repeat what the person is saying. Most listeners find this a tough thing to do. Usually the listener wants to jump in and explain how they solved a similar problem. Advice is appropriate when a person asks for help. But normally people just want to be heard. If we don't give them our full attention, their message can get lost. Try giving your full attention both at home and at work to improve communication.

Body Language and Nonverbal Communication

Management consultant Peter Drucker wrote, "The most important thing about communication is to hear what *isn't* being said." Baseball legend Yogi Berra said, "You can observe a lot by just watching." The magnitude of these two statements is overwhelming. Research points to the importance of nonverbal communication and tells us that only 7% of what we say has an impact on others. The remaining 93% is related by what we do *not* say, such as gestures, facial expressions, and voice tone. Which has more influence? Many people think communication consists only of words. Observing others' nonverbal language is an important skill to learn if we aim for success—to achieve our personal best.

What do you reveal to others before you open your mouth? Is it confidence or insecurity, strength or weakness? I realize that the attitude you project depends somewhat on who you are with, and what you are experiencing that day. Finish this sentence: "When people meet me for the first time they think I am ___." If the answer is "shy," and you really are an outgoing person, ask yourself what behavior you could change to give a more accurate impression of yourself. If you answer "snobby," and you are a warm person, look within to find out why people are misreading you. Ask someone you trust to give you clues to relate a positive impression of yourself. Try to be as open and as receptive to others as possible. People will reach out more to those who seem flexible and caring, rather than to those who appear rigid and aloof.

Have you heard the concept that a person's eyes are the windows to their soul? When you look at a person for one second you notice him or her as a human being. When you look at a person for three seconds you notice him or her as an individual. I will never forget a conversation I had with a woman who came up to me at the end of an intense keynote speech and said, "Joyce, I really loved your words, and I am now aware of roadblocks I have set up in my own life, but you didn't look at me once." Over 1,000 people filled the auditorium and this individual felt neglected. The power of eye contact cannot be overstated.

The tone of our voice also sends a message. People with strong voices get noticed the minute they speak. Those with softer or weaker voices are often ignored. We seem to have remote controls in our heads today; if you don't catch our interest early, we just turn you off. We need to capture others' attention. Listen to your favorite newscaster or actor. Most of them have had voice lessons to help them sound appealing and credible. Many people use speech coaches to help make their voices sound more powerful.

Take this quiz on verbal and nonverbal communication:

1. Do I realize that even if an idea is clear to me, it may not be clear to another person?

2. Do I make sure I fully understand what another person has told me before I reply?

3. Am I understanding of others' feelings, knowing that they may be different from my own?

4. Am I sensitive to someone else's point of view before judging that person's message?

5. When I communicate, do I ask questions to clear up any misunderstandings?

6. Do I understand that once a person feels understood, he or she tends to be less aggressive and less defensive?

7. Am I careful not to prejudge others by their appearance and manner of communicating?

Are you surprised by your answers? Most people feel that after they answer these questions they can improve their ability to communicate. It is important to assess your strengths as a communicator, and determine where you need to improve.

Body language and the tone of your voice convey much about your message and deserve investigation. This knowledge will improve your personal presentation and ability to observe and interpret others. We now know the power of active listening and nonverbal language. Let's put these two skills into practice to improve our networking skills.

Networking Strategies

According to the *American Heritage Dictionary*, a network is defined as, "An extended group of people with similar interests or concerns who interact and remain in informal contact for mutual assistance or support."[8] Networking can range from job leads or prospects, career decisions, referrals for health care, use of the Internet, etc. Many people have a fear of networking, yet it is an indispensable tool for professional success. Give as much as you can to networking in order to receive the most benefit from it.

As children we were taught not to talk to strangers. As we enter the business community and attend social functions, we are thrown into a room with people we have never met. Now what should we do? There may be cliques. Some may gather in groups and exclude us. Many of our school age fears of being excluded return in adulthood. Understanding the importance of networking, in your personal and professional lives, will assist you in your enjoyment during the process. It can be a real win-win situation.

Experts tell us that people are lonely because they build walls around themselves instead of building bridges to each other. When we communicate successfully we build bridges. We make connections that enable ideas to flourish and actions to occur.

Many networking skills are basic, yet people seek out refresher courses in networking techniques. At a business meeting or social gathering, carry your business cards with you and make sure they contain clear information about you. You want people to know what you do and how to contact you. Adjust your attitude so you will have fun and a good time. Practice your handshake. Business associates are surprised that some people still don't use powerful handshakes. Rehearse a 30-second self-introduction and be ready to use it. Compile a list of questions you want answered, or people you want to meet. Healthy relationships begin with clarity; they last only as long as we continue to invest in them.

When I attend the National Speakers Association convention, I prepare a list of marketing questions I want to ask, speakers I want to meet, and technical problems I seek solutions to. If possible, I set up appointments before the conference begins. I also make myself available for those new to the speaking business.

At a networking function, make sure you mingle with people you don't know, instead of always being with people you are familiar with. Be a host, not a guest. Do you know people who are insulted because they were not introduced to someone they wanted to meet? Don't wait for someone to greet you. Take the initiative. I found a message in a fortune cookie that read, "None of the successes of life work unless you do." Introduce yourself to someone standing all alone. You may make a friend for life. People remember those who help them. Recall Emerson's law of compensation, "You must give to receive."

Make sure you follow up with new contacts after the session or meeting is over. Someone has to make the first move. Set a lunch date or send the literature you promised. Over time you will build relationships with people from this type of forum. I have heard many success stories of people meeting at events and forming long term business relationships as a result of networking. These ideas could be what's missing for people who have no luck with networking. We make our own luck. Try these new ideas to help you prepare for and use networking.

Across the nation, people ask me for techniques on starting a conversation. Begin by reading newspaper sections you usually don't read, like the fashion or sports pages. You may not be an expert at either, but reading about an unfamiliar topic will give you a chance to know what others are talking about instead of just standing alone and feeling uninformed. A good conversationalist:

- Talks on a broad range of subjects and is well informed.
- Shows interest in what other people do for a living.
- Adjusts to the person with whom he or she is talking.
- Looks straight into the eyes of the person with whom they are conversing.
- Does not interrupt.
- Knows how to pay, and accept, compliments gracefully.
- Makes a shy person feel included in the group.
- Is aware when listeners become bored.
- Does not burst somebody else's bubble with negative comments.
- Addresses everyone in the group, not just one or two people.

Here are three examples of "openers" you can use if you fear starting a conversation with strangers:

1. Make an observation such as, "This is a great turnout. I've never seen so many people attend this meeting before."
2. Ask a question. "Is this your first time here? Are you a member?"
3. Self-disclosure. "I'm really looking forward to this speaker. I've heard him/her before and he/she gives valuable information."

Remember, we need to feel the fear (of networking, public speaking, etc.) to work through it.

Being visible is another important aspect of networking. You never know when you will meet your next boss, client, friend, or spouse at a party or meeting. Above all, be more interest*ed* than interest*ing*. The next time you talk with people, they will probably ask you questions about your life. Be humble, ask questions about others, and don't monopolize the conversation. When you meet someone who only talks about themselves, don't take it personally. Be assertive, take a deep breath, politely interrupt, and change the focus of the conversation to a more relevant topic. British novelist, Oscar Wilde said, "When people are wrapped up in themselves they make a pretty small package."

Presentation Skills

Fred's face turns red. He is panic-stricken. He is told he must make a speech to his peers. Fred, and many others, experience anxiety when asked to make a toast at a wedding or talk at a child's school function. You too may be asked to make a presentation in the coming years. Here are some simple tips to make these situations easier.

Making a presentation is a learned skill that improves with practice. Early in his political career President John F. Kennedy put his hands in his pockets to hide his nervousness when he had to speak in public. First Lady and United Nations delegate, Eleanor

Roosevelt, fainted at her first speech. But she came back strong.

Presenters admit to a wide range of mistakes. Inappropriate teasing is one—such as the speaker who told lawyer-bashing jokes without realizing the CEO and the president of the company were both attorneys. Talking too quickly or too slowly alienates audiences, as does boring people with a monotone voice. Not having enough knowledge about the topic is usually very apparent.

None of these dilemmas need occur. Making a presentation can be successful. Here are my favorite strategies for preparing and making powerful and successful speeches:

1. Know your audience. Place the spotlight on the source of your biggest anxiety, your audience. Research their needs, their problems, and their goals.

2. Build rapport. How are you and your audience alike? When people have things in common they tend to feel more comfortable.

3. Have fun. This will relax you and your audience.

4. Give yourself a pep talk. Being nervous is normal. Others are nervous too, but some hide it better than others.

5. Relax before, during, and after the presentation. Take a deep breath and look at the audience before you say your first word. This relaxes you and shows you have control, even though the butterflies are fluttering in your stomach. No one can see what's going on inside you.

6. Organize your speech. Your audience will appreciate an orderly presentation.

7. Know your purpose. Are you going to inform, inspire, or persuade?

The opening of your speech should comprise approximately 15% of your time, the body 75%, and the closing remarks about 10%. Use your opening remarks to grab their attention, build trust and credibility. Add interesting elements to hook the audience. In the body of your speech use facts, quotes, challenging questions, and personal stories. Give facts that show you know more than your audience. In your closing remarks, summarize, tie back into the opening, and suggest that your listeners take action. The most significant aspect of making a presentation is to be yourself and to talk to your audiences like they were your friend.

Effective presentations can enhance your personal life also. There will be toasts to make at weddings and roasts to make at parties. Your friends and relatives are rooting for you. What a missed opportunity for others if they don't hear your special message. Many helpful books and tapes on this subject await you at your local library or bookstore.

Clear communication is essential to excel in this pressure-filled world. Your home and work life will improve when you actively listen to others. People love to be heard. Be interested and you'll be more interesting. Notice your body language. Is it open and relaxed? Networking and presentation skills are techniques that will help you stretch your communication skills. Feel the fear and work through the anxiety the next time you make a presentation or attend a meeting.

In order to achieve your personal best you must get up just one more time than you fall. Take more opportunities to meet new people. Show them what a great person you are. Don't wait for your ship to come in, swim out to it—the water's fine! Go full speed ahead!

Work Sheet
Chapter 5

Face-to-Face Communication

This work sheet will help you think about how you communicate with others face-to-face. Read the entire list, then circle the skills you would like to improve upon. Tackle them, one at a time, and celebrate your new techniques.

1. Be brief, concise, and get to the point.
2. Be forceful and definite, rather than hesitant and apologetic.
3. Talk in specifics; give examples and details.
4. Tell compelling personal stories.
5. Let others know when you don't understand something they've said.
6. Let others know when you like something they have said or done.
7. Let others know when you disagree with them.
8. Let others know when you are getting irritated.
9. Listen to understand rather than thinking about your next remark.
10. Ask others what they are feeling rather than assuming you know.
11. Talk in group discussions.
12. Be able to tolerate silence with others.
13. Accept help from others.
14. Stand up for yourself.
15. _____

Action Plan
Chapter 5

Communication: It's a Two-way Street to Build Rapport

When you discover new ideas, or ways of performing a task better, write them down. It has been found that if new ideas aren't used within 24 hours, they are generally forgotten. Make a copy of this plan and place it in a prominent location in your home or office. Make sure you try all of the things you have made note of.

1.＿＿＿＿＿＿＿＿＿＿＿＿＿＿＿＿＿＿＿＿＿

2.＿＿＿＿＿＿＿＿＿＿＿＿＿＿＿＿＿＿＿＿＿

3.＿＿＿＿＿＿＿＿＿＿＿＿＿＿＿＿＿＿＿＿＿

4.＿＿＿＿＿＿＿＿＿＿＿＿＿＿＿＿＿＿＿＿＿

5.＿＿＿＿＿＿＿＿＿＿＿＿＿＿＿＿＿＿＿＿＿

Top performers are people who realize need to express their feelings. They confront ambiguity by asking questions for clarification. They do not wait for others to approach them. They take responsibility for their relationships by communicating in a direct and open style. What are your strengths when communicating with others?

＿＿＿＿＿＿＿＿＿＿＿＿＿＿＿＿＿＿＿＿＿＿

＿＿＿＿＿＿＿＿＿＿＿＿＿＿＿＿＿＿＿＿＿＿

＿＿＿＿＿＿＿＿＿＿＿＿＿＿＿＿＿＿＿＿＿＿

＿＿＿＿＿＿＿＿＿＿＿＿＿＿＿＿＿＿＿＿＿＿

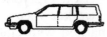

Chapter 6

Diversity: Even Hondas, Volvos and Chevys Can Get Along

Visualize a world filled with people just like you. They look identical to you, have the same skin tone, color of hair, and eyes. They are the same height, the same sex, age, and share the same interests and hobbies. What kind of world do you think this would be? Boring! Living in a homogeneous world would be a nightmare, yet some people seem to want just that.

To achieve the success we are capable of, personally and professionally, we must learn to appreciate the differences in each other. That statement sounds simplistic. It is. But simple does not mean easy. Diversity is recognizing, appreciating, valuing, and using the unique talents and contributions of all individuals, regardless of their differences. Differences include race, gender, age, language, weight, physical abilities, height, religion, technical and non-technical skills, marital status, education, sexual orientation, geographical background, birth order, values, work longevity, and even eating habits.

Workshop exercises show how we are different, even when we look the same, by virtue of different value systems. It is vitally important to understand others different from us. I have taken this program around the country and the positive feedback I have received has been overwhelming. At times people put on blinders and don't face the realities of their prejudice. This chapter is a mini-version of my diversity workshop.

The workplace is definitely changing and the changes will have a significant impact on everyone. Twenty-five years ago, the average worker was 29-years-old, male, white, local, and married with children. Women of that time generally worked in the home or part-time elsewhere. The women who worked outside the home were usually teachers, nurses, or secretaries. Older workers were considered smarter, and people with disabilities were not routinely found in the workplace.

Today, only 7-10% of the families in the United States fit the traditional "Ozzie and Harriet" model of a father who works, a mother who stays at home, and 2.4 children. In the year 2000, white males are predicted to comprise only 15% of incoming employees. About 60-65% of females over the age of 16 will work outside the home. Women will make up 47% of the workforce contrasted with 29% in 1950. They will probably place their children in day care centers. Employers who want to remain competitive during the next century will have to understand the unique needs of their ever-changing workforce. By understanding diversity and including everyone, companies will increase their bottom line.

Once America was known as the melting pot of the world. This view has proved to be inaccurate. Not only is it impossible to melt or fuse together the many diverse groups that make up the American workforce, most individuals are not willing to blend. A melting pot is the wrong metaphor.

Rather, think of the United States as a healthy tossed salad—a fresh, wonderful collection of colors, textures, and flavors. When everything is blended together the ingredients are no longer distinctive. Today's work-force is comprised of different minorities retaining their own identity. Therefore, we need to be sensitive to each other's needs. We need to treat *all* people with respect and dignity as individuals.

Much confusion is generated in today's workplace because some people turn to the old "we versus they" game. This creates all kinds of conflict and detracts from successful team building ideals. Americans differ in numerous ways. As individuals we were formed by a complex blend of variables: our ancestors' value systems, personalities, energy levels, and much more. Even siblings, people who grew up in the same house, can be quite different.

Different equals different. Different does not equal wrong. Workshop participants share with me how this statement helps them cope in this changing world.

Businesses that hope to thrive in the 21st century need to think about the importance of diversity now. Forward-looking businesses know that a good mix of employees will increase their bottom line. The customer base is changing along with the workforce. Businesses need to be aware that techniques which worked in the past may not necessarily work now or in the future.

New studies compare companies employing a diverse workforce with those who don't. The results are not surprising. A diverse workforce increases sales, growth, and performance. In the past we distrusted differences. Now, companies with a vision are teaching employees that differences are a valuable resource. Just think how much our family relationships would improve if relatives would be more accepting of each other, instead of making rash judgments and wounding the self-esteem of family members.

Consider these ground rules on diversity for use at home and in the office:

- There are few totally right or totally wrong answers.
- Listen to each other.
- Respect differences in others.
- Agree that it is okay to disagree.
- Speak for yourself.
- Contribute honestly and positively.
- Have fun.
- Different equals different, different does not equal wrong.

I once had the pleasure of sharing the speaking platform with Olympic gold medal gymnast, Mary Lou Retton. Her coach, Bela Karolyi, also coached Romanian gymnast, Nadia Comaneci. Mary Lou explained how the coach had to learn to treat her and Nadia differently because they were distinct people. Mary Lou drew energy from the spotlight and applause. She was fired up by competing with others in the Karolyi gym. Nadia was motivated by the passion of excellence and perfection, not the encouragement from the crowd. Two diverse women each needed a unique approach to bring out their best.

We need to treat others the way they want to be treated, not how we think they should be treated. We also need to express our individual needs to have those needs met. We benefit by learning the needs of the people with whom we live and work with. Although not always easy to accomplish, it is definitely worth trying. What a revelation you will have when you understand and appreciate others' differences.

Let's concentrate on some challenges we face when we are with people different from ourselves. We often judge, show prejudice, and stereotype other people.

Judging Others

We make rash judgments about people and situations before we have enough information. We tend to fill in the blanks haphazardly. My husband Jerry told me a story about a man stranded in the desert, desperately looking for water. He came upon a salesman yelling, "Ties for sale, ties for sale." The thirsty man thought the tie salesman was peculiar indeed, but continued searching for water. The next day, the thirsty man, crawling on hands and knees, weak and unable to walk, encountered the salesman again, shouting, "Ties for sale, ties for sale." By now the man was so weak he ignored the salesman. Suddenly he saw a restaurant on the horizon. The man crawled inside and was greeted by the host who announced, "You will need a tie, Sir, before we can serve you." How often do we make judgments before we know all the facts?

Enjoy this essay titled *First Thoughts*.

You and I, we meet as strangers, each carrying a mystery within us. I cannot say who you are. I may never know you completely. But I trust that you are a person in your own right, possessed of a beauty and value that are the Earth's richest treasures. So I make this promise to you; I will impose no identities upon you, but will invite you to become yourself without shame or fear. I will hold open a space for you in the world and allow your right to fill it with an authentic vocation and purpose. For as long as your search takes, you have my loyalty.[9]

---

[9]Reproduced from *A Workshop for Managing Diversity in the Workplace* by S.K. Kogod. Copyright ©1991 by Pfeiffer & Company, San Diego, CA. Used with permission.

I usually read this essay at the beginning of a training session which prompts an interesting discussion. One man explained how his company judged him negatively because he doesn't play golf. He doesn't want to spend time away from his young family to take golf lessons, yet he knows that some of his peers joke about him. Another person said she is a vegetarian and brings tofu to work. She is ridiculed as a "health nut." Her coworkers are not aware of the fact that she has cancer and is experimenting with a new diet.

Betty (not her real name), used to be very critical of others. She couldn't sleep well, had stomachaches and was angry most of the time. She sought a counselor for help. The first, and hardest task, was to stop judging others. When she ceased criticizing others, her stomachaches and sleeping problems subsided. Her circle of friends is beginning to grow again because she now accepts differences, and most importantly, she accepts herself. What an important lesson she learned—we didn't all come over on the same ship, but we are all in the same boat.

Do you ever feel badly for being different or unique? Recently I was challenged by a moment of doubt about my own uniqueness. I was being myself and having a great time at a dinner party. I was energetic, off the wall, and a little zany. Out of the blue one of the guests said, "Joyce, chill out!" What I heard was "Joyce, you're too much, too strong, too passionate, too intense!" I internalized this and started to doubt myself.

Several days later my daughter was thanking me for the "gifts" I have passed onto her: her raspy voice, her Mr. Magoo vision, her bow legs, and her addiction to chocolate. I said, "Wendy, tell me something good that I have given you." She whispered in my ear, "Your intensity, Mom." I said, "Seriously, Wendy, tell me one good thing." She replied, "Mom, my intensity made me valedictorian of my high school class, my intensity earned me several promotions at work, and my intensity gives me the passion, commitment, and the perseverance to go after my dreams." My self-doubts began to vanish. My uniqueness is the greatest gift I have. Know your uniqueness. Trust that it is your strength and live it freely. Different equals different. Different does not equal wrong.

To raise your level of compassion:

- Set aside snap judgments.
- Understand and remind yourself of your attractive features and why someone may like them.
- Give yourself permission not to approve of everything you see.
- Be open, expand your view, and gain insight.

I encourage people to watch a television show that they detest and practice the above techniques. The audience usually groans at this suggestion. They often experience a new and interesting awareness, however, when they view the program.

Prejudice

I ask workshop participants if they have experienced any kind of prejudice. Almost all raise their hand. After we establish trust among the group, the discussion usually becomes very intense. People learn they may look and sound differently, but share common experiences.

The following attitudes can signal problem areas you may experience at work or with friends:

- The world consists of us and them.
- We are right; they are wrong.
- We are good; they are bad.
- We are beautiful; they are ugly.

Prejudice thrives on hatred, fear and ignorance while pretending innocence. Discrimination and oppression are present everywhere. Hostility and violence can be destructive results. Do you see these symptoms in yourself? In your friends? If so, then maybe it's time for a tune-up. People need to be aware of the fact that the world is changing and outmoded behaviors cannot survive into the next century. Here is a simple, yet strong, technique to help you deal with a friend or business acquaintance who uses inappropriate language, "I really care about you as a friend (or acquaintance). I would appreciate it if you would not use those words when I am with you." Make the other person aware that these expressions or words are not acceptable in today's diverse world. Will Rogers wrote, "We will never have true civilization until we have learned to recognize the rights of others."

Stereotypes

Stereotypes don't appear out of the blue. Many times they come from our upbringing and old family baggage. Stereotypes induce negative feelings, block out information, and cloud judgment. We fill in many blanks with stereotypes. We cling to them for convenience, to avoid expending effort to learn about someone we don't understand. We can overcome stereotyping by being nonjudgmental, and more accepting. Instead of stereotyping, listen and pay attention to the specifics at issue.

Stereotypes get in the way of a diverse workforce. Some employees don't want to change and don't understand why it is necessary to get along better with others. Some people will not change until forced. They may like the status quo. Why rock the boat when their way has always worked in the past? One book or one workshop will not erase stereotypes, judgment, and prejudice. Time and effort are required to change attitudes that have been with us since childhood. Realizing that my way may not be the only way is a monumental task for some. Fortunately, we *can* change.

Adult attitudes promote stereotypes, especially among young people. We influence future generations. By criticizing our children, they learn to condemn. If our children live with hostility, they learn to fight. Yet, if we teach our children tolerance, they learn to be patient. If we teach them security, they learn to have faith in themselves and others. If we teach friendliness, our children learn that the world is a nice place in which to live.

Some of us grew up with parents who encouraged us to expand friendships and learn from variety. Other parents instilled fear by limited associations. Attitudes take time to change. Some people refuse change. The newspapers report about radical groups and clans that still exist and display blatant prejudice. Visualize the future of our changing world. What can we do to insure peace and harmony?

We have looked at existing problems, and the options we have. Now we need strategies to effect change. These tips will help you deal with an inappropriate joke, or being in the minority group at a social or business function.

Sometimes you will be in the dominant culture or group. Will you realize that others have fresh ideas and different perspectives to bring to your life or organization? Will you coach others on how to succeed? Will you apologize when you have offended someone from a different background?

Other times you will not belong to the dominant group. If you are rejected, will you still take pride in yourself? Will you realize you may have to learn new information and skills to succeed with others? Will you share what you learned about other people with those more like you? Will you resist blaming the dominant group for everything that goes wrong?

Some consider themselves "change agents." They challenge others who tell jokes which are racist, sexist, gender-related or otherwise offensive. They refrain from repeating rumors that reinforce prejudice or bias. They avoid generalizations like "all blacks are . . . ," "all disabled are . . . ," or "all men are . . . ." Change agents care about people different from themselves.

Advocates for change ask for an explanation of racist or inappropriate jokes. They push for the explanation until people are uncomfortable. Usually the jokester will avoid telling offensive jokes after that. Others confront a person privately when they feel the joke or comment was improper. The most important step is to not let the person get away with it; do something. If you leave the room in the middle of an inappropriate story or joke; the jokester will usually get the hint. You can say "ouch" when a person says something distasteful. People need to know when they are being offensive. Will Rogers said, "I don't think I ever hurt any man's feelings by my little gags. I know I never willfully did it. When I have to do it to make a living, I will quit."

Some people are fed up with "politically correct" language. At times people can go too far to make every expression acceptable to everyone. This real estate article, which appeared in the *National Enquirer*, and written by Steve Plamann, is an example of politically correct gone too far.

> What do the terms "walk-in closet," "master bedroom," "handy-man's special" and "perfect for children" have in common when used in real estate ads? Incredibly, they're illegal!
>
> "That's because they imply discrimination," explained Renee Allison, legal counsel for the California Newspaper Publishers Association.
>
> "The maximum fine for breaking the law—which is federal—is $50,000."
>
> Real estate agent Gizella O'Neill of San Jose, California, fumed: "In ads I can't use common sense terms everyone understands.
>
> "I had to pull a rental ad that said, 'Large yard—perfect for children.' The reference to children,

lawyers said, could be seen as discriminating against people who didn't have children. It's ludicrous!"

If your ad uses "master bedroom," you face a fine for being racist and sexist.

Use "walk-in closet" and you're in trouble, because you're implying that people who can't walk, can't use it.

In Oregon, there are some 140 unacceptable words and phrases listed in the Fair Housing Manual of the state's Newspaper Publishers' Association. These include: "able-bodied," "healthy," "quiet tenant," "responsible" and "single."

In Pennsylvania, forbidden words include "exclusive," "mature," "seniors," "mother-in-law suite" and "executive buyer."

If you are a female student looking for a female roommate and you don't want a male drug addict, you can't say "female," "student," or even "no drug addicts" without risking a fine.

Said Allison: "Drug addiction is considered a disability under federal and state law!"[10]

The world is changing and companies that train employees on sensitivity and diversity will gain global appeal. Celebrate events that honor diversity. At day's end, reflect on diverse events and people in your life. Learn to appreciate these differences. Use change and diversity as a wonderful opportunity to learn and grow.

No one is perfect and biases may slip off our tongues occasionally. Be aware of your own prejudices and try to understand their origin. Challenge yourself to examine assumptions and beliefs, then make the necessary changes.

Nature's beauty comes in all colors. The strengths of humankind take many forms. Every human being is wonderfully unique. All of us contribute in different ways. When we learn to honor the differences, and appreciate the mix, we'll find harmony.

---

[10]Reprinted with permission by *National Enquirer.*

Work Sheet
Chapter 6

Appreciating the Strengths in Diversity—What an Opportunity!

Diversity/Change Agent Quiz

1. Do you challenge others privately when they make racially, ethnically, or sexually offensive comments? Yes __ No __

2. Do you challenge people publicly when they make fun of others because of their race, gender, ethnic background, religion, appearance, disability, or sexual orientation? Yes __ No __

3. Do you think about the impact of your comments and actions before you speak or act? Yes __ No __

4. Do you avoid using language that reinforces stereotypes, such as, "You're acting like a pack of wild Indians!," "Jew them down.," "White of you.," and "I'll get my girl to do it."? Yes __ No __

5. Do you learn about people different from yourself, by reading, attending seminars, watching TV specials, etc.? Yes __ No __

6. Do you value people who are different from you as a resource because of their unique skills, abilities, perspectives, and approaches? Yes __ No __

7. Do you disregard physical characteristics, disabilities, attractiveness, height, weight, dress, etc., when interacting with others and making decisions about their ability? Yes __ No __

Action Plan
Chapter 6

Diversity: Even Hondas, Volvos and Chevys Can Get Along

When you discover new ideas, or ways of performing a task better, write them down. It has been found that if new ideas aren't used within 24 hours, they are generally forgotten. Make a copy of this plan and place it in a prominent location in your home or office. Make sure you try all of the things you have made note of.

1._____

2._____

3._____

4._____

5._____

Top performers are people who realize the value of team building. They understand and appreciate the benefits of being with people who are different from themselves. What groups do you belong to where team members are different from you? How have these differences been beneficial to you?

_____

_____

_____

_____

_____

_____

Chapter 7

Creativity: Discover the Back Roads to Develop Your Creative Genius

Creativity is the ability to look at the same things everyone else does, but to see things differently—to find the hidden connections between the facts and create something completely new. It is like changing a lens or the focus on your camera. That something may be as grand as a classical symphony or as simple as a new way to arrange your desk to be more productive.

In order to succeed in today's competitive and highly pressurized society, we need to see and do things differently than we have ever done before. You may think everything seems just fine at your workplace, or at home. It is your challenge to find the things in your life that might be improved.

Donald Trauscht, CEO of Borg-Warner Corporation said, "It's a marathon race. Some people will sail across the finish line. Others will fall by the side of the road." I remember an interview I heard from the 1992 Summer Olympics in Barcelona, Spain. A commentator asked athlete Jeanne Vickers why she changed her strategy in the middle of the Olympics. The commentator was surprised because Jeanne always ran her race the same way; her method was tried and tested. Jeanne replied, "I got here, looked at my competition, and knew if I did my best I wouldn't be among the winners." Our philosophy at Joyce Weiss Associates is that the best can only get better.

This chapter will help you find and use your creativity to enrich your life. Any of these ideas can be used at home or work. Creativity will spice up your existence plus improve the morale of your associates.

During my workshops only a few people usually raise their hands when I ask the question, "How many of you are creative?" Some people assume that they have to draw, paint, sculpt, sew, or write poetry to be creative. But we are all born with creativity. *The magic inside you is no hocus pocus. Set your goals and you create the focus.* Does this statement look familiar by now? Creativity is not the exclusive property of geniuses, but an outlook, a set of skills and habits *anyone* can develop. The type of people willing to stretch the rules and look for a second right answer will succeed.

A plain iron bar is worth $5. If you forge horseshoes from that iron bar, the value increases to $10.50. If it is made into needles, the price rises to $3,285. And if you make springs from it, its worth increases to a whopping $250,000. The difference between $5 and $250,000 is creativity.

What stops us from pursuing creativity? Certainly you have heard some of these comments before:

- It won't work.
- A leopard can't change its spots.
- Who do you think you are?
- If it were possible, someone else would have done it.
- You can't teach an old dog new tricks.

- What will happen if the project fails?
- Just let it be, don't rock the boat.
- Yes, but . . . .
- We tried that before.
- We've always done it that way.

These are "killer" phrases. They immediately stop people's creative thinking. We still hear the following statements in today's workplace:

- Don't waste time thinking.
- That is really a stupid idea.
- Don't be ridiculous.
- I don't get paid to think.
- That's not in my job description.
- Your idea is too ahead of the times.

The following is a real-life story that shows the importance of pursuing your creative ideas. Not too long ago, a bright young man wrote about a potential venture he created for a college business course. The professor wrote on the paper, "Your ideas are too unrealistic, please stick to our guidelines for the project." Fred Wilson, the creator and founder of Federal Express, was the student. His idea was to deliver mail within 24 hours. His service provides an important asset to businesses today. He didn't let this professor destroy his idea.

In 1905 Ernest Hamwi sold waffles at the World's Fair. When he noticed people were getting bored and wanted something new he folded his waffles and put ice cream inside. The rest is history.

There are thousands of stories like these. One could be yours. Remember to keep the creative juices flowing—especially when someone tries to sabotage your idea. This has happened many times in my life, too.

Years ago, people chided me and said I would never be successful as a professional speaker because I was a woman and the profession was too new. People said speaking was not a "real" job and I would be wasting my time and energy. Today more than 3,500 professional speakers in the United States belong to the National Speakers Association. A speaking career is an important one; we help people achieve their goals and succeed in life. I'm glad I followed my dreams. American writer David Thoreau wrote, "If you have built castles in the air, that is where they should be; now put foundations under them."

We often place mental blocks in our way that inhibit our creativity. Let's look at some examples.

MENTAL BLOCK 1—FOLLOW THE RULES

Sometimes we become more creative by *ignoring* the rules. Polish astronomer Copernicus disproved the theory that the earth is the center of the universe. Napoleon found another way to fight a successful military campaign. 20th century Spanish artist Pablo Picasso conceived another use for the bicycle; he removed the seat and handle bars and welded them together to create his famous bull sculpture. Many people were taught not to color outside the lines. More than one right answer exists.

Some people feel more comfortable following the rules than challenging them. Some professionals in today's unemployment line still firmly believe that keeping a low profile and not making waves are the best ways to keep your job. But times have changed. Jobs and business depend on innovation. In order to succeed people have to look at new ways of doing things. If they don't, they may be left behind, jobless. I know a very talented woman who was asked to leave her company. Management told her she had all the right stuff to make it there but she didn't venture beyond the rules. They wanted employees unafraid to think independently. They gave her job leads and an outstanding reference. They knew for their company to survive and thrive, they needed creative employees. Keep asking yourself how you can get better. You may be at the top of your success ladder, and I send my congratulations. Realize that to stay there you need to grow and improve constantly.

MENTAL BLOCK 2—BE PRACTICAL

Of course being practical is business savvy. But it can be a weakness if stretched too far. Think about the following statements and have fun discussing them in group situations: What if people were born old and grew young? What if electromagnetic disturbances made all television reception impossible? What if dogs were intelligent and kept people as pets? These "what if" questions are impractical, yet they start people thinking beyond their limited barriers and can spark new creativity and insight.

MENTAL BLOCK 3—TO ERR IS WRONG

Most people think that success and failure are opposites; however, they are products of the same process. After a mistake, wise people wonder how to avoid making the same error again. Explorer Christopher Columbus erred while looking for a shorter route to India and discovered the Americas. Inventor Thomas Edison knew 1,800 ways *not* to build a light bulb, yet he eventually succeeded. We learn from trial and error, not by doing things the same way each time. If you are original, you will be wrong a lot of the time. Progress always involves risk; you can't steal second base with your foot on first.

Thomas Watson, the founder of IBM, said, "The way to succeed is to double your failure rate." If you make an error, use it as a stepping stone to a new idea you might not have otherwise discovered. Strengthen your risk "muscle." Every person has one, but you have to exercise it or it will atrophy. Take one risk, small or large, every day.

MENTAL BLOCK 4—PLAY IS FRIVOLOUS

Play is actually crucial. During what kinds of activities do you get your ideas?

- When you are faced with a problem.
- When things break down.
- When there is a need to fill.
- When you are playing around.
- When you are not taking yourself too seriously.
- When awakened in the middle of the night.
- While exercising.
- During a boring meeting.
- While showering or shaving.

Physicist Albert Einstein said, "Make friends with your shower. If inspired to sing, maybe the song has an idea in it for you."

Play is inspirational and helps our creative juices flow. Author Roger Von Oech wrote, "Necessity may be the mother of invention, but play is certainly the father." Your mental blocks are loosened during play. It doesn't matter what is right and wrong in play. Children don't know all the "have to's" and "should's." Plato wrote, "Life must be lived as play." Make your workplace and home life a fun place and watch the creativity bubble up.

MENTAL BLOCK 5—THAT'S NOT MY AREA

I hear this excuse throughout the business world today. My question to those people is, "If it were your area, what would you do?" Try to recall the last time you heard "that's not my department," or "that's not my job" when you were a customer. Didn't it make your blood boil? Just think how our clients feel when they hear that expression. My daughter Wendy expects poor service; if she gets good service, she is elated. She is generally irritated by the terrible attitudes from some people in service industries. Her new way of thinking has saved her from getting upset since she is motivated by excellence and quality.

MENTAL BLOCK 6—I AM NOT CREATIVE

We need to recognize our talents that we have taken for granted in the past. These are usually the skills that bring out our creativity. Decorating a home, putting together a colorful wardrobe, telling wonderful stories, cooking delicious meals, planting a beautiful garden, keeping a family or department together (especially during challenging times), and writing interesting articles, are just a few of the talents people often take for granted. If you say to yourself, "I can't do that!," you are not thinking creatively. Decide what would happen if you *could.*

Successful athletes visualize themselves winning before the competition begins. They run a mental movie through their minds over and over. This creative way of winning builds confidence. In belief there is power. Our eyes are opened. Our opportunities become clear and our visions become realities. When teams are in a slump, it is usually because they are reliving failures in their minds.

Here's a wonderful example of desire conquering defeat. Two frogs fell into a bucket of cream. The first frog, seeing no way to get his footing in the thick white liquid, accepted his fate and drowned. The second frog didn't like that approach. He started thrashing around in the cream and doing whatever he could to stay afloat. After a while, all of this churning motion turned the cream into butter, and he was able to regain his footing and hop out. Do you see how valuable creativity can be?

MENTAL BLOCK 7—DON'T BE FOOLISH

Candid Camera, a brilliant and funny television program aired this scene in 1960: A man waits patiently for an elevator in an office building. When it arrives the doors open. He notices that everyone is turned around facing the rear. He steps in and he faces the rear of the elevator too, with his back to the doors, even though there was no reason for doing so.

All of us are subject to peer pressure. I have witnessed a phenomenon in the workplace called "group think." It stops people from being creative. Sometimes people "agree to agree" just because they believe their boss thinks a certain way. New ideas do not develop in a conformist environment. I did the following "group think" experiment in a workshop. An idea was suggested and everyone loved it. The group voted and the idea was passed. I suggested the decision be postponed for one week to study it further. Sure enough, the group changed its mind and vetoed the idea based on their belief that I didn't agree with their decision.

"Group think" can be very subtle at times. People may not know it is happening. Be aware of it and watch for it among your coworkers. Sometimes people don't want to go against the ideas of the boss or majority. Unfortunately, this kind of corporate culture dampens all creative spirits. This "group think" mentality can exist at home as well.

I tell a story at the beginning of every one of my workshops on creativity. It shows how we need to rid ourselves of our mental blocks in order to move on in our lives. A Zen master invited a student to his house for tea. He poured fresh tea into the student's cup, and continued pouring, even after the cup was full. The tea overflowed and spilled onto the floor. The student yelled, "Master, you must stop pouring the tea, it is overflowing my cup." The master responded, "That's very observant of you. The same is true with you. If you are to receive any of my teachings, you must first empty out what you have in your mental cup." I go a step further and ask participants to return to the ways they used to think when they were children: open, nonjudgmental, curious, constantly learning, and funny.

Charles Kettering wrote, "When I was the head of research at General Motors and wanted a problem solved, I'd place a table outside the meeting room with a sign: 'Leave slide rules here.' If I didn't do that, I'd find someone reaching for his or her slide rule. Then he or she would say, 'Boss, you can't do it.'" While we seldom see slide rules today, thinking mired in cement continues to exist. Before you dismiss any idea as impossible, find at least three good reasons why it *can* be done.

Now that we have some ideas about what hinders our creativity, I would like to explore how to find the creativity within. There may be another right answer. You can be creative if you let go of old ways of thinking. Thomas Edison wrote, "If we did all the things we are capable of doing, we would literally astonish ourselves."

The great former Boston Celtics forward Larry Bird was filming a soft drink commercial in which he was supposed to miss a jump shot. He sunk nine baskets in a row before he could compel himself to miss one. He had conditioned himself over the years to win. When the ball hit his hands, he automatically went through a pattern of motion that put the ball through the hoop. Realize that you and I can condition any behavior if we do it with enough repetition. It was very hard for Larry Bird to break his habit of success.

Many businesses today have gone through paradigm training. Paradigms are sets of rules that establish or define boundaries. They tell you how to behave inside the boundaries in order to be successful. Paradigms tell you there is a game and how to play it. A paradigm shift is a change to a new game, a new set of rules. I ask workshop participants to discuss what problems they want to solve, but have no idea how to begin to do so.

Ask yourself what seems impossible to change in your work or home that would create fundamental reorganization. It may seem impossible because the solution is outside your boundaries. But the exercise makes you step beyond your perceived limitations to look for answers. This is an important lesson to learn. It helps us break away from the philosophy of "this is how we have always done it."

In her book, *Atlas Shrugged*, author Ayn Rand said, "All work is creative work if done by a thinking mind, and no work is creative if done by a blank mind who repeats in uncritical stupor a routine he has learned from others. The quickest way to kill the human spirit is to ask someone to do mediocre work."[11]

Creative people maintain an open, imaginative mind. Seeing all possibilities, and how to achieve them, marks the power of imagination. Your imagination stands as your own personal laboratory. Here you can rehearse the endless possibilities, map out plans, and visualize overcoming obstacles. Imagination turns possibilities into realities.

Playwright George Bernard Shaw wrote, "You see things and you say, 'Why?' But I dream things that never were, and I say, 'Why not?'" American writer and reformer, Louisa May Alcott wrote, "Far away, there in the sunshine, are my highest aspirations. I may not reach them, but I can look up and see their beauty, believe in them, and try to follow where they lead." Publisher Malcolm Forbes declared, "When you cease to dream, you cease to live."

Another quality creative people share is responsibility. The fulfillment of your dreams lies within you and you alone. When you understand and accept this, then nothing, or no one, can deny your greatness. The power to succeed or fail is *yours*. No one can take that away from you.

If you are excited about the new ideas you have read in this book, but fail to change the things in your life that you would like to change, *nothing* will hap-

---

[11]Excerpt from *ATLAS SHRUGGED* by Ayn Rand. Copyright © 1957, renewed 1985 by Ayn Rand. Used by permission of NAL, a division of Penguin Books USA Inc.

pen and the ideas will vanish. A motivational expression I often hear is, "If it's going to be, it's up to me." The day we take total responsibility for everything we do, is the day we'll succeed . . . to go full speed ahead.

Excellence is a quality that is vital for people who want to achieve their personal and professional best. Excellence is going far beyond the call of duty—doing more than is expected. That's what it's all about. It consists of maintaining the highest standards, looking after the smallest details, and going the extra mile. Excellence means doing your absolute best in everything, in every way.

United States Army General George Patton said, "If a man has done his best, what else is there?" President Abraham Lincoln wrote, "I do the very best I know how, the very best I can, and I mean to keep on doing so until the end." American novelist Thomas Wolf said, "If a man has a talent and cannot use it, he has failed. If he has a talent and uses only half of it, he has partly failed. If he has a talent and learns somehow to use the whole of it, he has gloriously succeeded, and won a satisfaction and triumph few men ever know." And Thomas Edison wrote, "If there is a way to do it better, find it."

Business managers ask how they can improve their staff meetings and enable their employees to be more creative. Use these ideas whenever you want to have an energetic, uplifting, and results-oriented brainstorming session. Some guidelines to help you begin are:

- Only make positive statements.
- Listen to other perspectives and different departments.
- Develop as many ideas as you can.
- Offer every idea you can think of, even if it seems silly.
- Don't criticize any idea.
- Ask what has worked in the past.
- Do something totally new and different.

- Have a fresh, childlike approach.
- Add humor and fun.
- Get excited about the ideas.
- Think of constant improvement.
- Make sure "killer" phrases are not allowed.
- Use igniting phrases such as: "Keep talking.," "You're on the right track.," "We can do a lot with that idea.," "Wow! Let's try it!," "It's sure nice to have you with us.," and "Look out world, here we come!"

These ideas will help you become more creative and reach your next level of success.

Training magazine tells us that five years ago, one out of twenty-five companies did creativity training. Now one out of three companies does so. They realize the potential of brainstorming to help their employees achieve their personal best.

Creativity is a never-ending adventure. It can take you places you've always dreamed of. It is fun to accomplish the difficult or the impossible; that is where there is less competition. If at first you don't succeed, take a break, then try again. If everyone says you're wrong, you're one step ahead. If everyone laughs at you, you are two steps ahead. Brainstorming meetings can play an important part in expanding our focus from individual performance to group creation.

As you can see, creativity is an important part of the equation for success. I repeat, creativity is not the exclusive property of geniuses, but an outlook, a set of skills and habits anyone can develop. Those who merely want to survive don't have to be concerned about imagination and vision. People who want joy and fulfillment will decide how they can stretch their imaginations beyond their wildest dreams. You *do* have choices about the future. Don't let your future happen by accident. Create a future that is wonderful, exciting, happy—and most of all—full of creativity.

Work Sheet
Chapter 7

Developing Your Creative Genius—Celebrate the Magic Within!

The Four C's of Creativity

Curiosity: There is always a better way! Play the "what if" game. What if people were born old and grew young? What If people slept 23 hours and were awake only one hour each day?

_____

_____

_____

_____

Courage: "Behold the turtle. He makes progress only when his neck is out!" Creativity means taking risks. What smart risks have you recently taken?

_____

_____

_____

_____

Climate: In a large business organization, creativity often is stifled if the boss is immune to change. How have you helped create a positive environment at home or work?

_____

_____

_____

_____

Commitment: List your most important goals and objectives. Can you pledge yourself to these goals? Will you give what it takes to carry out these objectives?

_____

_____

_____

_____

There is a difference between interest and commitment. When you are interested in doing something, you do it only when it's convenient. When you are committed to doing something, you accept no excuses, only results.

Action Plan
Chapter 7

Creativity: Discover the Back Roads to Develop Your Creative Genius

When you discover new ideas, or ways of performing a task better, write them down. It has been found that if new ideas aren't used within 24 hours, they are generally forgotten. Make a copy of this plan and place it in a prominent location in your home or office. Make sure you try all of the things you have made note of.

1._____

2._____

3._____

4._____

5._____

Top performers are people who realize they must constantly improve. They know that stagnation is an indication of the need to change and grow. What are you doing differently today than you were doing one year ago? How do you constantly improve at home and at work?

_____

_____

_____

_____

Chapter 8

Risk-taking and Goal-setting: Create Your Own Road Map

What is a dream? It is a fond hope. What is a goal? It is an objective. What is a risk? It is a chance of loss. These words play a role in each person's life. When you have dreams, goals, and risks—it shows. And if you don't, that also shows.

Over the years I have consulted with many people about their careers. I ask them what advice they give to others just starting out. The simplicity of their answers is fascinating. They suggest:

- Take risks early on in your career.
- Have the courage to chase your dreams.
- Have a plan of action, and review it each year, to make sure you are headed in the right direction.

Taking risks and setting goals are topics that people talk a lot about, yet many times neglect to take the necessary action. This chapter will cover the importance of taking risks, why people fear risk, and how to find the courage to take more risks in order to excel in this pressure-laden world. You will learn how to use goal-setting strategies to turn your dreams into magnificent realities.

Did you ever think about how a lobster grows when its shell is so hard? A lobster instinctively knows when its body is cramped and sheds its shell at regular intervals. It looks for a safe spot to rest while the hard shell comes off. Its pink membrane becomes the next shell. Obviously, the lobster is vulnerable without its protective shell. It can be thrown against a coral reef or eaten by other sea creatures. The lobster risks its life in order to grow.

We can learn valuable lessons from lobsters—we too must grow and change. We know when our shells have grown too tight. We become angry, frightened, bored, stifled, or find life very dull. Some people continue to smother in old shells, no longer productive. They feel safe. But nothing new ever happens to them. Others are luckier. In order to grow, they realize they must shed their shells of complacency and take risks. With risk comes vulnerability. I invite all of you to shed last year's shell—despite the dangers associated with it—and get ready for new, exciting adventures.

Actor Alan Alda said to his daughter, "Be brave enough to live creatively. Your creativity is a place no one else has ever been. You have to leave the city of your comfort. Go into the wilderness of your intuition. You can't get there by bus, only by hard work and risk, and by not quite knowing what you're doing. What you'll discover will be wonderful. What you'll discover will be yourself."

Why do we fear taking risks? What keeps us stuck in our routines? Take a look at six risk busters:

1. People are often bound by habits and comfort. They feel they have no control and don't realize

they *are* capable of change. They think negative thoughts such as:

- I am too old.
- My skills are not up to date.
- I am not happy in this line of work, but at least it's a job.
- I will never find another mate.

People limit their vision with these negative messages.

2. Others resist change because they follow the "must" and "should" rules. For example: "Everyone in my family is a teacher. I should follow in their footsteps." When we use these words it shows we feel guilty about our actions. A workshop participant once said, "I tell people not to 'should' on me."

3. People don't take risks because they are afraid of looking foolish or making mistakes. Every artist spoils a canvas occasionally. Every accountant uses the delete key on the computer and a pencil with an eraser. No baseball player ever had a batting average of 1000. You cannot allow your mistakes to stop you. The person who never makes a mistake is the person who never accepts challenges. She or he merely survives and never thrives. Many businesses are hiring risk takers to help their company grow.

4. People are often stymied in their lives or careers because they don't resolve the personal issues that make them unhappy. They complain about things, yet don't work to improve their situations. Of course, it's easier to complain than to accept responsibility. It is easier to blame someone else than to examine patterns in our own behavior that hinder our success. One gentleman complained that he always marries the wrong kind of woman. He recently married for the eighth time. I suggested he look within for patterns in his choice of wives. He

was not open to my suggestion; he would rather continue to play the "blame" game.

5. Fear of the unknown is another risk buster. We have all heard or used the following expressions:

- I'm not ready yet.
- I might fail.
- I don't know enough.
- Someday, when I have everything in order, I will make the change.

Do you remember your first day of high school or college? Your first day of camp? You were probably scared, but also excited and full of anticipation. Conquering fear feels much the same. You must be ready to walk into unfamiliar territory and leave behind your safe, reliable, comfort zone. Fear is a part of growing. We will always fear the new and unknown to varying degrees. Look back at what you feared one year ago. And ten years ago. Do those fears seem small and trivial today?

For some people, failure is worse than death. If you need to worry about something, think of the opportunities you miss when you don't try. The good thing about failure is that it inspires no jealousy! British poet Rudyard Kipling wrote, "We have forty million reasons for failure, but not a single excuse." Some people have thousands of reasons why they *cannot*, when all they need is *one* reason why they *can*. If something is worth doing, it is worth doing poorly on the first attempt.

6. Lack of support is another reason that some people stay stuck in one place. They don't know what to do because they have not brainstormed with others. The power of networking was explored in an earlier chapter. Networking can be very influential. Many success stories come from clients who have talked with others who share similar experiences.

They support each other with job leads and make suggestions to network with other professionals.

What methods can we use if we want to excel? One of the first steps is to recognize obstacles you may be placing in your path. Share these risk busters with others having difficulty breaking their patterns of fear and failure.

Colonel Harlan Sanders was 65 years old when he opened his first Kentucky Fried Chicken outlet. He had just received his first retirement check and decided upon this new venture. He assumed everyone loved fried chicken, so he went about trying to sell his recipe. His idea didn't work at first; people were not interested. Did that stop him? You know the answer, and the rest is history. KFC has become a world-renowned success story.

Some people think every change has to be dramatic, such as sky diving or walking on hot coals. This is not so. Whether you seek a promotion, ask someone for a date, move to another location, or start a new business, it involves risks. Once you understand how they work, you will be able to take smarter risks. Use these three stages of risk-taking to make intelligent choices:

STAGE 1—PREPARE AND PLAN FOR RISK.

Fear helps us prepare. It is important to confront the unknown at this time. Ask yourself what, or who, is holding you back? This is also an excellent time to assess potential losses. Realize you can get hurt; weigh the pros and cons. What specifically are you afraid of losing? Is it security or money? What would you do if the bottom fell out? How can you limit your losses? Can you get out of the situation before the worst happens? Ask questions about your plan.

STAGE 2—MAKE A COMMITMENT TO TAKE RISKS.

This is the point of no return—putting the plan into action. No more just talking about it. It's time to put the pedal to the metal and go for it. The *American*

Heritage Dictionary defines commitment as "The state of being bound emotionally or intellectually to a course of action. . . ."[12]

STAGE 3—EVALUATE YOUR ACTION STEPS.

Complete the plan of action. You broke away from the old pattern. You took the risk, now evaluate it. Many people do not reach this important stage. They allow fear and doubt to take over. Dr. David Viscott, one of America's foremost common sense psychiatrists and author of the book *Risking,* wrote, "If your life is ever going to get better, you'll have to take chances."

We examined the importance of taking risks. Now how can we get the courage to take more risks? Eleanor Roosevelt said, "You gain strength, courage and confidence from every experience. You must stop and look fear in the face. You must do the thing you think you cannot do." Spanish novelist Cervantes penned, "He who loses wealth, loses much. He who loses a friend, loses more. But he who loses courage, loses all." Success is never final. Failure is never fatal. It is courage that counts. Newspaper columnist Ann Landers said it all when she wrote, "If I were asked to give what I consider the single most useful bit of advice for all humanity, it would be this: expect trouble as an inevitable part of life and when it comes, hold your head high, look it squarely in the eye and say, 'I will be better than you. You cannot defeat me.'" We've all heard stories about people overcoming great obstacles in their lives, whether they are about a physical illness or a personal struggle. Success can be attributed to courage, strength, and hope. Will Rogers said, "Nothing makes a man broad-minded like adversity." And Mark Twain wrote, "Courage is resistance to fear, master of fear, not absence of fear." Remember, success does not come to *you.* You go to *it.*

---

[12]Copyright © 1992 by Houghton Mifflin Company. Reprinted by permission from *THE HERITAGE DICTIONARY OF THE ENGLISH LANGUAGE, THIRD EDITION.*

Quotes like these have helped many people, especially when things looked bleak. Use index cards to capture some of the quotations throughout this book. Carry them with you or display them on your refrigerator, mirror, or desk. Inspirational quotes reinforce the idea that we need courage to take risks, no matter the outcome. Things usually turn out better, but it takes courage and patience to see the results.

British playwright George Bernard Shaw wrote, "The people who get on in this world are the people who get up and look for the circumstances they want, and if they can't find them, they make them." And Victor Hugo wrote, "People don't lack strength; they lack will." Taking risks is a characteristic that separates people who just survive from those who achieve their personal best.

GOAL SETTING.

It's now time to put all these wonderful ideas on risk-taking into action. Setting goals is a powerful strategy that helps you achieve the things you want. Some examples are:

- I will lose 10 pounds by summer.
- I will find a worthwhile job in a year.
- I will improve my marriage by meeting with my partner one hour each day, five times per week.
- I will make more time for myself.

All of these goals sound great. But there is a difference between people who just say the words, and those who put their words into action. A good example is a story about Mary, who had just met George. She said to him, "You look like my third husband." George asked, "How many times have you been married?" Mary smiled and said, "Twice." This woman knew how to dream, was motivated, and put her thoughts into action. Mary had all the right qualities for successful goal setting.

Having a strong commitment *and* an intense desire are prerequisites for setting goals. A lack of desire means a key ingredient to success is missing. Many talented individuals fail because they lack desire. Many victories have been snatched by the underdog because he or she had more desire to win than the front runner. If you desire intensely, and you act upon it, then everything stands within your reach. As Walt Disney, animator and film producer, told us, "All our dreams can come true if we have the courage to pursue them." Abraham Lincoln said, "Always bear in mind that your own resolution to succeed is more important than any other one thing." The truly motivated person knows that obstacles are a part of any game plan. But if you have an intense desire to do something, you *will* find a way to get it done.

An important key to success in reaching your goals and dreams is the ability to see opportunity everywhere. There are no limits to our opportunities. Most of us see only a small portion of what is possible. We create opportunities by seeing the possibilities, and having the courage to act upon them. Opportunities are always there, but we must look for them. Author Napoleon Hill wrote, "Opportunity often comes disguised in the form of misfortune or temporary defeat." We need to turn obstacles into opportunities. Albert Einstein said, "In the middle of difficulty is opportunity." It is hard to see opportunity during challenging times, but if you look for it, it will appear. Remember, *The magic inside you is no hocus pocus. Set your goals and you create the focus.*

The purpose of setting goals is to focus our attention. Our mind cannot focus until it has clear objectives. The magic begins when we set goals. Then the switch is turned on, the current begins to flow, and the power to accomplish becomes a reality. "People with goals succeed because they know where they are going," observed Earl Nightingale, professional speaker.

An important step in getting what you want out of life is to decide exactly *what* you want. (Please read that sentence again.) When I worked as a guidance counselor, I dealt with people wanting to change careers. People who came in with ideas about what they wanted to do had the most success. When someone walked in saying, "I will do anything, just find me a job!," I knew it would be a long tough journey to place this client in a satisfying position.

Eleanor Roosevelt said, "The future belongs to those who believe in the beauty of their dreams." And Swiss psychiatrist Carl Jung wrote, "Your vision will become clearer only when you can look into your own heart. Who looks outside, dreams. Who looks inside, awakens." These insightful words from Lewis Carroll's *Alice in Wonderland* ring true. Alice asked the Cat, "Would you tell me, please, which way I ought to go from here?" "That depends a good deal on where you want to get to," said the Cat. "I don't much care where—" said Alice. "Then it doesn't matter which way you go," said the Cat. "—So long as I get *somewhere,*" Alice added as an explanation. "Oh, you're sure to do that," said the Cat, "if you only walk long enough."[13]

Here is an easy outline for putting ideas into action:

Analysis—Identify those areas you want to explore. Group brainstorming is valuable during this stage.

Goals—Identify the specific goals you want to achieve. These can include challenges you want to face or opportunities you want to pursue.

Ideas—Generate all the ideas and solutions which could help you meet your goals.

Selection—Analyze, identify, and select those ideas which are most likely to help you achieve your goals.

---

[13]From Lewis Carroll's *The Complete Works of Lewis Carroll*, pages 71 and 72, The Modern Library.

Action—Implement those selected ideas, make them reality. People who aren't successful in achieving goals may not know the actual steps to take. It's easier to talk about doing something than to take the necessary actions.

The character Dagny Taggart states in Ayn Rand's *Atlas Shrugged*, "We don't tell, we show; we don't claim, we prove." Her brother Jim says, "You should have been born about 100 years earlier, then you would have had a chance." "To heck with that," Dagny responds, "I intend to make my own chance."[14]

My son Ron often tells me, "I'm not just here for the ride. I'm here to drive." He is always challenging himself by doing such interesting things as running a marathon, scuba diving, or becoming a licensed airplane pilot. He "walks his talk."

We all know people who simply exist. There are so many exciting experiences in life. We need to learn to seize the day. Will Rogers wrote, "Even if you're on the right track, you'll get run over if you just sit there." Former automotive executive Lee Iacocca said in a Chrysler commercial, "Do something. Lead, follow, or get out of the way." And Rita Jones, my marketing genius, repeats an old saying, "Good things happen to those who wait. Great things happen to those who get out of their chair and go for it."

The following plan will help you take action toward reaching your goals. I use it in many of my workshops. Ask yourself:

- Where do I want to be in one year?
- What will I have to do to get there?
- What risks will I have to take?
- What is the best outcome?

[14]Excerpt from *ATLAS SHRUGGED* by Ayn Rand. Copyright © 1957, renewed 1985 by Ayn Rand. Used by permission of NAL, a division of Penguin Books USA Inc.

Think and act positively; this could make the difference in your success. Create a positive statement that defines your dreams. State it as if it has already happened, such as:

- I weigh 125 pounds and I feel in control.
- My marriage is strong and it feels wonderful again.
- I received my promotion and feel very proud of myself.
- My appointment book is full and I enjoy referring business to others.

Repeat your statement over and over throughout your day, especially when facing an unpleasant situation. Write it on paper and display it in a prominent place. Let it be your private mantra, your joyous chant of expectation. Don't be fooled by the simplicity of this. Try it. Even if it seems silly or hopeless at first, stick with it. It works!

A final thought on goal setting; be careful what you ask for, you just might get it. Actor Cary Grant said, "I've grown into the person I wanted to be." What a positive thought.

It is important to look at our lives in as simple of terms as we can. Think how you would answer the following question: What is something you can brush your teeth with, sleep on, and sit on? If you answered a toothbrush, a bed, and a chair, you answered correctly. Those who tried to think of one item for all three were making it more complicated than it needed to be.

We often live our lives in a more complex manner than we need to. The simple truth is, the people who will achieve their personal best know one thing for certain: the magic to follow their dreams is within themselves. There are those who wait for their future to come to them and those who create their future.

You can do anything and everything you set your mind to . . . to go full speed ahead. The question is: Will you? You can, if you keep the following in mind:

- Channel stress into positive energy.
- Gain control of your life . . . who's in charge anyway?
- Accept responsibility for your life.
- Take your life seriously and yourself a little lighter.
- Communicate openly and with power to earn the respect you deserve.
- Appreciate your uniqueness and the differences in others.
- Use your creativity, at home and at work, to celebrate the magic within.
- Take more smart risks.
- Set your goals.
- Turn your dreams into magnificent realities.

At his 1961 presidential inaugural address, John F. Kennedy said, "All this will not be finished in the first 100 days. Nor will it be finished in the first 1,000 days, nor in the life of this administration, nor even perhaps in our lifetime on this planet. But let us begin."

We cannot always control what goes on outside, but we can control what goes on inside our lives. I challenge you to go beyond safety and have the courage to make mistakes, to learn, laugh, and grow. Live your dreams. Others have done it. You can too!

Work Sheet
Chapter 8

From Here to There

Purpose: Bringing about change in our personal lives is often a difficult and complex undertaking. Many constraints may stand in the way and must be removed before we can achieve our personal goals. This strategy is designed to help you get in touch with some of the things you would like to change about yourself, what your new goals might be, and some of the risks, constraints, and consequences that are involved.

From Here ➜	To There	Risks/Constraints Consequences
A	B	C

- In window A, draw a picture of something you would like to change about yourself.
- In window B, draw a picture of what you would like to be after the change.
- In window C, draw a picture of a barrier or constraint which might stand in your way and/or a risk which might be involved if you actually tried to make the change.

Work Sheet
Chapter 8

Risk-taking and Goal-setting:
Create Your Own Road Map

Putting Goals into Action

1. Where do I want to be in ___ years?

_____

_____

_____

_____

_____

2. What will I have to do to reach that goal?

_____

_____

_____

_____

3. What risks will I have to take?

_____

_____

_____

_____

4. What is the best thing that could happen to me?

_____

_____

_____

_____

Action Plan
Chapter 8

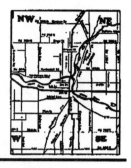

Risk-taking and Goal-setting: Create Your Own Road Map

When you discover new ideas, or ways of performing a task better, write them down. It has been found that if new ideas aren't used within 24 hours, they are generally forgotten. Make a copy of this plan and place it in a prominent location in your home or office. Make sure you try all of the things you have made note of.

1._____

2._____

3._____

4._____

5._____

Top performers are people who realize that lifelong learning is the only way to stay fresh and motivated. They invest in their own growth and development. List the ways you stay motivated and grow. What books, tapes, or classes would you like to avail yourself of? Which ones would you recommend to others?

_____

_____

_____

_____

_____

_____

Suggested Reading

Albrecht, Karl. *The Creative Corporation*. Dow Jones-Irwin, 1987.

Barker, Joel Arthur. *Future Edge: Discovering The New Paradigms of Success*. William Morrow & Company Inc., 1992.

Benson M.D., Herbert. *The Relaxation Response*. Avon Books, 1975.

Canfield, Jack and Hansen, Mark Victor, *Chicken Soup For The Soul*. Health Communications Inc., 1993.

Cassidy, John and Rimbeaux, B.C. *Juggling For The Complete Klutz*. Klutz Press, 1977.

Garfield, Charles. *Peak Performers*. Avon Books, 1986.

Hart, Michael. *The 100 Most Influential Persons In History*. Citadel Press, 1994.

Johnson, William. *Workforce 2000*. The Hudson Institute, 1987.

Josefowitz, Natasha. *Is This Where I Was Going?* Warner Books, 1983.

K-Burr, B. *Creating Champions*. Ivane Publications, 1991.

Klein, Allen. *The Healing Power Of Humor*. Jeremy P. Tarcher Inc., 1989.

Kriegel, Robert. *If It Ain't Broke . . . Break It!*. Warner Books, 1991

Laborde, Genie Z. *Influencing With Integrity*. Syntony Publishing, 1994.

McGartland, Grace. *Thunderbolt Thinking*. Bernard-Davis Productions, 1994.

McNally, David. *Even Eagles Need A Push*. TransForm Press, 1990.

Metcalf, C.W. & Felible, Roma. *Lighten Up: Survival Skills For People Under Pressure.* Addison-Wesley Publishing Co., 1992.

Michalko, Michael. *Thinkertoys: A Handbook Of Business Creativity For The '90s*. Ten Speed Press, 1991.

Nelson, Bob. *1001 Ways To Reward Employees*. Workman Publishing, 1994.

Roane, Susan. *How To Work A Room*. Warner Books, 1988.

Robbins, Anthony. *Unlimited Power*. Simon & Shuster, 1986.

Sembler, Ricardo. *Maverick: The Success Story Behind The World's Most Unusual Workplace*. Warner Books, 1993.

Sheehy, Gail. *New Passages: Mapping Your Life Across Time*. Random House, 1995.

Viscott M.D., David. *Risking*. Pocket Books, 1977.

Give this Gift of Excellence to Your Friends and Colleagues

Check Your Leading Bookstore or Order Here

☐ **YES**, I want _____ copies of *Full Speed Ahead* at $16.95 each, plus $3 shipping per book (Michigan residents please add $1.02 state sales tax per book). Canadian orders must be accompanied by a postal money order in US funds. Allow 15 days for delivery.

☐ **YES**, I am interested in having Joyce Weiss speak or present a workshop to my company, association, school, or organization. Please send information.

☐ **YES**, I am interested in receiving information on Joyce Weiss' video *I've Fallen And I Can Get Up*. This video helps people turn obstacles into opportunity while giving a presentation.

☐ **YES**, I am interested in receiving information on Joyce Weiss' audio cassette *Dealing With Difficult People*. This tape shows individuals how to deal with negative people, calm them down, and gain control.

My check or money order for $_____ is enclosed.
Please charge my ☐ Visa ☐ MasterCard

Name _____

Phone _____

Organization _____

Address _____

City/State/Zip _____

Card # _____

Exp. Date _____Signature _____

Please make your check payable and return to:
Bloomfield Press
P.O. Box 250163
West Bloomfield, MI 48325-0163
Fax: 810-682-0358

Or call your credit card order to: 1-800-713-1926